The MYSTERIES of SAN CLEMENTE

WAYNE BRAUDRICK

STONE TOWER PRESS
stonetowerpress.com

Stone Tower Press
7 Ellen Road
Middletown, RI 02842
stonetowerpress.com

Paperback ISBN: 979-8-9852553-2-4

Formatting and cover design by Amy Cole, JPL Design Solutions

The cover image: Choir stall, Basilica San Clemente, www.alamy.com

Personal photographs taken inside Basilica di San Clemente were taken many years ago before photography was prohibited.

Printed in the United States of America

Dedicated to John Anderson, who first went there with us, and Rick Wroten, who made it possible for me to study repeatedly in Rome.

HIGHEST LEVEL OF BASILICA DI SAN CLEMENTE

Less than a 5-minute walk from Rome's Colosseum stands a lesser-known structure of equal and perhaps even greater importance for Christianity. Overlooked by most tourists and only recently appreciated by historians, the Basilica di San Clemente may hold important clues to the early history of Christianity. This multilayer site also sheds light on medieval tensions between Latin Christianity in the West and Orthodox Christianity in the East. Further, one of the great mysteries in St. Paul's famous *Epistle to the Romans* seems to be revealed many feet beneath the existing basilica. Come explore the mysteries of San Clemente in these pages. You may be surprised at your discoveries!

CONTENTS

PROLOGUE

THE LIVING WATER

I hear the fresh spring water rushing by on its way to the Cloaca Maxima. As the irrepressible sound bounces off walls built two thousand years before my birth, I feel both old and young at the same time. There are certain places—places where important events have occurred—that seem to achieve this ageless effect. This is such a place.

The sound of the water has always been here, joined by spray from other splashes through the centuries. Before the Roman Republic (509 BC to 27 BC) installed the Cloaca Maxima to drain the swamp, this spring ran like a ribbon of living water through the malarial infestation that comprised the lower parts of the city. Once this room was built, servants used the luxury of the running water to prepare meals feverishly for leaders of the Republic. Here, pagan libations were dutifully poured out on the carefully laid bricks. Early Christians gathered here to pour wine for their *agape* feast. The physical and spiritual family of an early martyr cried out their tears behind the relative security of these walls. And over and through it all the spring kept flowing.

They built more than a room around the spring. A large building, possibly the main mint for Republican Rome, was erected. After the mint was moved, the building fell to the control of a wealthy wing of the Flavian family, conceivably serving as a home for Titus Flavius Clemens—who was a consul, nephew of the Roman Emperor Vespasian, and a cousin of the emperors Titus and Domitian. The more than 10,000 square feet of space became a place of great import for many people on many levels—among them, the earliest Christians.

Pictured is subterranean water flowing beneath the lowest level of San Clemente, viewed through an opening in the original corner room of the facility (what de Rossi called "the kitchen"). Photo by Janna Braudrick

There is history as well as mystery in the stones of this building. This site teaches a great deal about the function and form of the earliest Christian churches. It also speaks to the development of the present-day Roman Catholic Church, exposes some of the struggles between the Eastern and Western Churches in the days before the Great Schism of 1054, and throws important light on St. Paul's 1st-century-AD writing of the *Epistle to the Romans*.

How staggering it is to realize that such a significant site was covered with rubble and trash, buried thirty feet underground, and completely forgotten for over a thousand years. The spring still flowed through the house, but no one noticed for a long time…

FR. JOSEPH MULLOOLY, O.P. (1812–1880)

CHAPTER 1

SAN CLEMENTE, THE FATHER, AND THE FOUNDER

As one might suspect from his surname, Father Joseph Mullooly, O.P., was an Irishman—an Irish Dominican priest. Though born in the Emerald Isle in 1812, Fr. Joseph was assigned to a parish in Rome. Since 1667, leadership of the titular Basilica of San Clemente was (and is still) the purview of the Irish Dominicans, and Fr. Joseph was assigned superior of San Clemente in 1852, an appointment that was to prove fortuitous.[1]

Father Mullooly meticulously cared for his church that dated from the 12th century. He protected and preserved everything from the ceiling frescoes to the famous floor. The Cosmati floor tiles of San Clemente are a treasure. For more than a hundred years spanning before and after the 12th century, four generations of the Cosmati family made and fashioned the tiles for many Renaissance churches, including the famous flooring of St. Peter's Basilica. Craftsmen of the highest order, the Cosmati had specifically dedicated their energy to creating the floor covering ordered for San Clemente, and the results are breathtaking.

Cosmati tile work in San Clemente

When the Cosmati tiles were in need of cleaning and repair, Father Mullooly hired the best craftsmen available. He even supervised them carefully, apparently cognizant of the enhanced work ethic induced by having a priest looking over one's shoulder.

Though no one recorded the dialogue, we can imagine the surprise when one of the workers discovered something underneath the flooring of the church. There appeared to be a large space beneath the church, with resonant echoes that indicated an enclosed construction. Though the considerable amount of rubble made any immediate diagnosis impossible, it was obvious that something was down there. Father Joseph determined to find out what.

However, four powerful blockades stood in Father Mullooly's path:

1. Many believed there was little of consequence to be discovered.

Completed in the early 12th century, Basilica San Clemente had been the sole inhabitant of this real estate for as long as anyone could remember. True, there were legends about St. Clement and early churches inhabiting the area, but few actually imagined there had been anything important beneath the floor of the beautiful church.

Of course, the entire area had been reclaimed from the swamps and settled during the era of the late Roman Republic.

The building of the Flavian Amphitheatre (now universally known as the Colosseum or Coliseum) two blocks down the street raised real estate values among the urban-conscious Romans, and the neighborhood became a posh enclave nestled among the Lateran, Esquiline, and Coelian hills. Of course, value wasn't the only thing that rose over the years. Most Romans in Father Mullooly's day understood that the street level in most parts of the city was significantly higher in the 19th century than it had been back in the 1st century. After the "barbarian" invasions, papal wars and banditti of the Middle Ages, the population of Rome had experienced significant decline. Unused sections of town became covered by centuries of build-up and the famous hills of Rome became mere rises in the ground, no longer precipitous heights between deep valleys.

This build-up is a truism of nearly every ancient or classical site around the world. Think of it like this: imagine that a child constructs a small house out of her Lego toys. If you placed that house outside and left it alone in your backyard for one year, what would form there? A small mound would build up over the house as dirt blew into the structure and grass grew over it. After a year, we would have what archeologists call a "tel." In certain places like Greece, Israel, and Jordan, the tels are quite evident, as layer after layer of civilization builds upon the ruins of the one before. In Rome, this is less obvious because the debris filled in between the hills.

The thinkers around Father Mullooly were not shocked that debris was found beneath the church building. In fact, that was to be expected. Even the columns inside St. Clement's (the Anglicized name is preferred by some of the Irish Dominicans who serve as stewards the property) display the continual recycling that is part of Roman building. Few of the columns match in color or size, and their capitals are quite diverse. They were salvaged from other old buildings and pressed into service for the "new" basilica in the 12th century. Thus, to find underfoot the presence of an apparently intact building was nothing particularly unexpected. Its potential size was certainly impressive and brought to mind certain partially-recollected legends regarding St. Clement himself and an older church in the valley between the Esquiline and Coelian Hills. Nonetheless, there was little excitement about a discovery that doubtlessly would lead merely to more old Roman trash.

We should note that if the basilica had lain outside the city limits, then the reaction would have been decidedly different. Outside the city, Enlightenment scholars, churchmen, schoolboys, and even ruffians were continuing to discover ancient underground burial sites known as catacombs. These discoveries were well-publicized and elicited much romantic response from across Europe and America, including Edgar Allen Poe's macabre piece set in the catacombs and titled *The Cask of Amontillado*. However, Father Mullooly's find was inside the walls and thus of minimal interest, as no Roman—Christian, pagan, or Jew—would have buried anyone but a pope inside the city walls.

2. Archaeology was in its infancy as a discipline.

Up to the time of Father Joseph, archaeology was a loose practice nearly devoid of any discipline. However, a few voices for scientific inquiry were being raised, especially in Britain and France. In Italy, there was only one great scholar dedicated to careful inquiry and excavation, Giovanni Battista (Carlo) de Rossi (1822–1894). So revolutionary in his careful methods was de Rossi that he became known as the founder of Christian archaeology. Father Joseph Mullooly wisely turned to de Rossi for help in understanding what lay beneath his church.

Though undisciplined in the mid-1800s, archaeology is actually an old practice dating back more than 2500 years. The last emperor of the Neo-Babylonian Empire, Nabonidus (r. 556 BC to 539 BC), became one of the earliest archaeologists. Nabonidus was an unusual king. He was utterly dedicated to Sin—the moon god. That may sound insignificant to us, but in Babylon, it was very politically incorrect. For 1000 years, the leader in the Babylonian pantheon of gods was Bel (also called Marduk) and his son Nebo. Bel/Marduk was god of the sun. Nebo was the god of wisdom. Nobody worshipped Sin anymore. Sin, the moon god, had been the old Sumerian chief deity earlier when the peoples were nomads who traveled at night. In the 500s BC, when Nabonidus reigned, the real power was believed to be in the sun god, Marduk, and the priests of his temple. The solar deity Bel had eclipsed the lunar deity Sin in popular devotion.

Nabonidus worshipping symbols of the god Sin,
Collection of the British Museum

But Nabonidus was committed to Sin. Things became so politically uncomfortable for him in Babylon that he abandoned the capital city and spent ten straight years on military campaign in greater Babylonia, Mesopotamia, and Arabia. During those years, Nabonidus became one of the first great archaeologists in history. He was fascinated with the past, and excavated historical sites in Ur, Uruk, and Agade—each of them associated with past worship of the god Sin.

The primary sites of excavations of Nabonidus
Map modified from the work of Chris Mundigler

The clay cylinder pictured on page 21 relates a dream of Nabonidus in which the god Sin commanded him to rebuild an ancient temple to Sin in Haran (also called Harran located in present-day southeastern Turkey). This temple had been in decay for over 500 years, since the days of Israel's King David. Further, the temple ruins lay in territory controlled by the Medes.

When Nabonidus's earlier predecessor Nebuchadnezzar ruled, the Medes had been subservient to the Babylonians. But by the time Nabonidus took the throne, the Medes constituted a real threat daily growing more anti-Babylonian. Yet, the god Sin told Nabonidus to move ahead with the temple construction, because a subordinate king named Cyrus would take over the Median Kingdom and Cyrus would be friendlier toward Babylon. In one sense, this prophecy came true. We know from history (including Daniel 5), that Cyrus did take over the Median Kingdom and he was interested in Babylon. He was so "friendly," in fact, that Cyrus ended up conquering Babylon and deposing Nabonidus and his son Belshazzar!

Cyrus Cylinder. Property of the Iran Museum, on loan to the British Museum

Thus, Nabonidus became not only the earliest committed archaeologist, but also the first reconstructionist when he rebuilt the ancient temple of Sin. Notice that his archaeological activity was fueled by his personal devotion to his god. Further, Nabonidus's work never involved what later experts would call a complete study; rather, he only looked into those places that could give him the answers he desired. That's why he only dug at sites where his favorite god had been worshipped.

Lions' Gate, Mycenae, Greece, photo by Janna Braudrick

The work of this last Babylonian king is illustrative because the discipline of archaeology had advanced little beyond his methods in the 2400 years that had passed from Nabonidus to de Rossi. Yet, there had been a few notable discoveries. The finding of Troy and excavation of Mycenae by Heinrich Schliemann had certainly brought archaeology some notoriety. However, Schliemann's work, like that of most 19th-century archaeologists, was plagued by loose-labeling, poor methods, and excessive showmanship.

Even when oddities existed in more modern buildings, Mediterranean peoples were disinclined to assume those oddities had specific purpose. For example, Basilica di San Clemente boasts odd structures at the floor level of the 12th-century church.

In some late-medieval buildings, brick arches are built in for support—a practice borrowed from classical times. However, these half-arches bear no great weight and appear superfluous. But in reality, they speak to something older beneath them, a message Carlo de Rossi heard and understood.

Wall of Basilica di San Clemente
Photo by Janna Braudrick

He was one of the first to effectively combat ignorance in the infant discipline and raise archaeology from a side-show of history to a science of investigative thinking. He became more than a mere fundraiser. De Rossi was a builder of lasting partnerships, writing in French and conversant in English and German in order to help his contemporaries comprehend Latin and the city of Rome. His masterwork, *La Roma Sotterranea Christiana* (Rome, 1877, Vols. I–III) was completed after his death and opened Rome to large numbers of tourists, students, and historians. It also became an important piece in the growing foundation of modern archaeology.

De Rossi and Father Mullooly—the founder of church archaeology and the father of the St. Clement parish—formed an unusual partnership and were dedicated to their joint venture of discovery. Such ardor proved necessary, given the third hurdle they faced.

3. The Vatican was not initially in favor of the archaeological work.

The reasons for the reticence in the Vatican have more to do with history and politics than with any anti-archaeological bent. Before Christianity became legal in Rome and the Roman Empire in the 4th century, churches met in private homes or leased buildings known as *tituli*. These house churches (*domus ecclesiae* in Latin sources) were known as *tituli* because they became connected with titled persons who owned or had access to the meeting house.

For example, the *Titulus Aemilianae,* presently the church of the Santi Quattro Cornati, was named for a member of the Aemilia family—one of the wealthiest and most important patrician families in Rome. The Aemilia could trace their roots back to the second king of Rome. Over the centuries, members held every important political office, provided a massive public basilica, and funded two major roads that bear their gens (family or clan) name to this day (the *Via Aemilia* and the *Via Aemilia Scauri*).

One of the fictions that persists in Christian history is the idea that the first century of Christians were almost exclusively poor. In actuality, the largest percentages to follow the resurrected Christ came from the upper classes of Greco-Roman society. The Gospels relate how wealthy people funded Jesus's "academy" with his disciples, some even following Him themselves. (e.g., see *Luke* 8:1–3.) The New Testament book *The Acts of the Apostles* specifies that a Christian gathering in Jerusalem met in the large gated house of Mary, a Jew possessing Roman citizenship. (See *Acts* 12.) Scottish archaeologist and New Testament scholar Sir William M. Ramsay (1851–1939) noted that this practice continued into the later decades of the 1st century, when large numbers of upper-class people believed in Jesus.

So, it is no surprise when a member of the gens Aemilia opens her large villa on the Coelian Hill for Christians to meet there. As noted above, the church built above that home is today known as Santi Quattro Coronati, or the Four Holy

Martyrs. It also is very old, the original construction dating from the 4th century. The structure of the large original villa, for centuries home of the *Titulus Aemilianae*, is still evident underneath the basilica.

Over time, the *titular churches* came to represent important points of power for the papacy. The medieval popes began a remarkably successful program of granting leadership of titular churches to priests and bishops from outside Rome. This eventually morphed into a mainstay of the modern College of Cardinals. By the time of Fr. Mullooly's discovery, Pope Pius IX was understandably sensitive to international attitudes toward the Holy See. Pius, the longest serving pope, spent much of his papal reign embroiled in political turmoil. He lost the papal states to Italian unification efforts, fiercely resisted Protestant evangelism by issuing papal bulls covering the dogmas of the Immaculate Conception and papal infallibility, and attempted Roman Catholic unification via the first Vatican Council. Despite all these challenges, Pius visited the work at San Clemente five times between 1857 and 1861. Though no one knows why he cooled toward the Clemente work, it is possible that he reasoned finding anything of controversy might set a spark to the political powder keg surrounding the papacy.

In short, four great forces were grinding against the Holy See: the growing movement to politically unify Italy, a hardening culture of disbelief in Christianity that had spread from universities such as those in Berlin into most of Europe, the personal progressive nature of Pius IX, and his desire to keep the Papal States under Vatican control.

All of this came to a head for the Vatican in the late 1850s when a well-intentioned citizen kidnapped a secretly-baptized Jewish boy, Edgardo Mortara, to ensure the child was raised Christian. The ensuing news coverage seemed to bring all four forces to bear against the papacy. Garibaldi and the Italian advocates of the unification movement saw an opening to promote national laws. Anti-Christian forces positively drooled over the embarrassment brought by this violation of accepted family convention. Pius IX himself was an advocate of better treatment of Jews, yet the anger directed against him and the threat of losing the papal states made him increasingly inflexible.[2]

This pressurized situation created an uneasy relationship between Pius IX and the political powers of Europe which led to friction between the pope and the city of Rome.

The condition of Rome in the latter 19th century is well described by Norwood Young in a 1901 travel guide. Young's unflattering and anti-Christian portrait details the lawlessness of a city scourged by banditti and shows how any novel action by the pope could inflame strikes and riots. Therefore, while the Vatican didn't officially restrict the initial excavations at San Clemente, neither did Pius IX offer much encouragement. In fact, his Commission on Sacred Archaeology withdrew all support in early 1861.

4. European Enlightenment thought had a curious relationship with history.

As the 18th century gave way to the 19th century, Enlightenment thought began to change. The foundations of the Renaissance and Reformation eras were grounded in the past, something that seemed restrictive to the new thinkers of Europe. From the *philosophes* of Paris to the theologians of Berlin, the past began to be used as a springboard for deconstruction instead of a foundation for edification. This required that truth be disassociated from hard fact and recast as speculation based on one's perspective.[3]

In such a milieu, a committed Dominican priest and an amateur archaeologist such as Fr. Mullooly appears as something between a laughable aberration and a threat to progressive thinking. What he discovered might make Christian foundations more reasonable. Thus, the popular intellectuals of Europe were as cool as was the pope toward the project, though from an exactly opposite point-of-view.

Father Mullooly's near contemporary, Sigmund Freud, serves as an ideal illustration. Freud's letters display an absolute fear of Rome, and he often uses the city as a metaphor for psychological issues. Freud also compared the human psyche to an ancient city where layers of architecture all rest atop the oldest constructions underneath. He expressed terror before his visit to Rome in 1901, haunted by all the layers and especially bothered at the idea of an absolute foundation that couldn't be completely understood. Of course, the anti-Semitism in Roman Catholic Christianity in Freud's day deeply troubled him as well. Apparently, Freud never set foot in St. Clement's, which is tragic. Not only would he have gained opportunity to really think through absolute and foundational history, Freud could have engaged with the legacy of Semites who found peace and prosperity in Messiah Jesus. We will delve into the Jewish history of San Clemente in chapter 3.

Middle level of San Clemente

Despite these challenges, the Father and the Founder kept digging. By 1870 they had exceeded any reasonable expectations, uncovering much of the 4th-century basilica and the amazing frescoes added to the walls up through the 11th century.

Digging deeper, they also uncovered a late 2nd-century Mithraeum, which we will discuss in the final chapter. Until his death in 1880, Fr. Mullooly remained a tireless defender of the archaeology and history embodied in San Clemente. He missed few opportunities to spread the word. Though his efforts never yielded the funding or interest de Rossi enjoyed over the catacombs work, Fr. Mullooly did make some powerful contacts.

For example, the British Empress Queen Victoria received a letter from her daughter Princess Alice dated 9th April 1873 concerning the basilica. She shared that Fr. Mullooly had shown her through San Clemente during her Grand Tour: "We visited San Clemente two days ago, and Father Mulooly [sic] took us through the three churches—one under the other." Joseph Mullooly was indeed a zealous host for the site, yet his endeavor struggled to gain the financial stability it needed and the fame it merited.

CHAPTER 2

SAN CLEMENTE AND CHRISTIANITY IN THE EAST AND WEST

A legend that seems to have begun in the 6th century concerns a late-1st-century Bishop of Rome who made a very important trip to the Crimean Peninsula. St. Clement, the bishop in question and namesake of the basilica, likely never made such a journey, but the story serves an important purpose. It displays how western and eastern Christians (or Latin Christianity and Eastern Christianity) viewed each other in the years leading up to their complete break in 1054—an event known as the Great Schism. Remarkably, Basilica di San Clemente stands as a witness to both Latin and Eastern Christianity.

Though the earliest sources regarding St. Clement mention no such trek to the east, that doesn't mean we can definitively say there is no basis for the story. To do so condemns one to the foolishness of materialist thinking that only considers what is clearly seen. That mindset not only eliminates learning from non-material truth, it cuts off undiscovered material things as well. For example, had Father Mullooly been closed to the unknown he would never have started digging under the floor of St. Clement's basilica.

The wisest way to proceed with unattested legendary information is to examine the elements of the story and see if clear connections to known facts emerge. With that in mind, consider the legend:

> Clement lived in Rome where he was a leader in one of the early churches in the capital city. According to some versions, he was the same person as Titus Flavius Clemens, a member of the imperial family. In other descriptions, he is a friend and fellow Christian laborer with Clemens. When Domitian ascended to the imperial purple as emperor (ca. AD 81.), he began the first systematic persecution of Christians. Clement was banished to the Crimean Peninsula on the Black Sea. (Later versions place Clement's exile to Trajan's reign, sometime before AD 117).
>
> Clement was condemned to work in a stone quarry, a punishment usually reserved only for slaves. There, he led numerous other workers to trust in Jesus. In some retellings, this involved God providing a miraculous spring in answer to Clement's prayer for water. As a consequence for spreading Christianity, Clement was martyred by being tied to a boat anchor and drowned in the Black Sea. Allegedly, every year, a miraculous ebbing of the sea at that spot near modern Sebastopol revealed a divinely-constructed memorial containing Clement's

> bones. Some add that a child once drowned at the spot, but when his lifeless body touched Clement's shrine, he was resurrected and jettisoned to the surface.
>
> An alternative legend states that Clement's bones were buried with an anchor, making no mention of drowning. The bones and anchor were deposited in caves near the village of Inkerman, leading to the later founding of the Inkerman Cave Monastery of St. Clement. Sometime around AD 867, St. Cyril and his brother St. Methodius made a pilgrimage to the site on their way to Rome. They brought Clement's bones with them to Rome.

Notice that the saga of St. Clement's journey east includes several intriguing elements:

- Persecution under the Roman Emperor
- Punishment suitable for a slave
- A memorial involving an anchor
- The bones of a Church Father making a long journey home

There appears to be some veracity to these aspects of the legends, though the whole versions appear unlikely (and in specifics, contradict each other). The first two bullet points will be considered in the next chapter. The latter two relate to the subject of this one.

Saints Cyril and Methodius

Saints Cyril and Methodius are two of the most important figures in eastern European history and theology. For their work as Christian missionaries, they are remembered as heroic figures dubbed "Apostles to the Slavs." Cyril is also very important in the story of the Basilica di San Clemente, where his name was Latinized from his native "Kyril" to "Cyril."

Brilliant and bold, these brothers were born in Thessalonica—Cyril ca. AD 827. and the elder Methodius around AD 820. Their father, Leo, served as a *drungarios,* a military rank used in the Eastern Roman Empire. Essentially a brigade commander, the *drungarios* falls in rank somewhere between the equivalent of a present-day colonel and a brigadier general. It was a position that allowed for some wealth, connections, and familial education.

Theoktistos, in the white cap, advises the Byzantine Emperor Michael III and his mother, the Empress Theodora. From the 13th-century History of John Skylitzes

Leo died when the brothers were in their teens, but his sons came to the attention of the eunuch priest and Byzantine official Theoktistos. Theoktistos had risen to great power and influence in the imperial court.[4] Under the Emperor Theophilos (r. 829–842), he was appointed head of the Public Post. More than a mere Postmaster General, this rank involved many duties including direction of most of the empire's foreign affairs. As the Emperor was dying, he made Theoktistos one of the regent council for his heir—the two-year-old Michael (Michael III). With adroit political capacity, Theoktistos shouldered aside the other regents and became *de facto* ruler of the empire alongside the Empress Mother, Theodora.

With power consolidating in his hands, Theoktistos initiated a series of wide-ranging moves. He engaged in warfare and diplomacy with Bulgars, Arab Muslims, Khazars, and even tribal peoples such as the Rus. On the whole, the warfare was unsuccessful and the diplomacy helpful. In early 843, he gathered a group of like-minded theologians and officials in his house where they held a private synod (a regional council) covering a number of ecclesiastical topics, especially focusing on the iconoclasm that had been state policy for almost a century. Today, that gathering is known as the Synod of 843.

Iconoclasm was a movement that attempted to reverse what some saw as idolatry among Christians. Particularly in the East, the practice had developed of kissing and bowing before images of Jesus, Mary, and famous Christians. In the early Middle Ages, the churches had taken to referring to these Christians as "saints,"

Section of the late-14th-early 15th-c. icon "The Triumph of Orthodoxy," British Museum. Empress Theodora and son Michael III stand on the left of a representation of the Hodegetria icon. (This famous icon displays Mary and Jesus, and late legend claims it was painted by St. Luke the Evangelist.) Methodios I anchors the right side with Theoktistos and iconodule bishops.

going beyond the biblical statement that all who trust Jesus are saints (e.g. *Romans* 1:7; *Philippians* 1:1; *1 Thessalonians* 3:13). Images of saints were painted on wooden panels and called icons ("image" in Greek). Those who opposed reverence toward icons were known as "iconoclasts."

Theoktistos's decision to reestablish icons in churches after more than a century of controversy was met with widespread rejoicing, especially from the Empress Mother Theodora, who had secretly prayed before icons despite her husband Theophilos's official iconoclasm. Because of the public support, Theoktistos and Theodora were emboldened to depose the Patriarch John VII.[5] John VII, who had earned the nickname "Grammatikos" for his great learning, was removed in favor of solidly iconodule (pro-icon) Methodios I—a famous abbot who had been imprisoned for championing icons. One week later, Theoktistos, Theodora, and Methodios I led a public procession to the Hagia Sophia church in Constantinople to re-install icons. The results of Theoktistos's Synod of 843 is still cause of rejoicing for modern Eastern Orthodox churches, and the re-establishment of icons is called "The Triumph of Orthodoxy." Understandably, the Orthodox Church recognized Theoktistos as a saint.

Just before the famous regional Synod of 843 that reaffirmed icons, Theoktistos was introduced to the young Cyril. He arranged for Cyril to receive an advanced education, possibly at state expense. Such was permissible because Cyril was considering the priesthood and because Theoktistos's policies had led to a large imperial budget surplus. It may have been at this time that Cyril adopted his ecclesiastical name for which he is known, his birth name having been Constantine. Similarly, his brother Methodius accepted that lasting name in place of his birth name, Michael. As with Cyril, the time of Methodius's name change is not clear, but it possibly occurred around 842 when Cyril was sent to obtain higher learning.

Cyril excelled as a student in Constantinople, flourishing under gifted teachers such as Photios and, as a result, he was offered numerous positions in both the state and the church. He chose the role of *chartophylax* in the patriarchal library at Constantinople—the greatest collection of information in the world. The *chartophylax* was an ecclesiastical official in charge of all records and documents, somewhat akin to an American Librarian of Congress or the Prefect of the Vatican Library. Sometime during this service, Cyril accepted holy orders as a priest. At least, that is the Eastern understanding. The Western version shows Cyril becoming a priest much later in Rome—a point of controversy discussed later. Methodius was ordained a deacon and became a well-respected abbot of a monastery in conjunction with some imperial administrative duties.

Befitting a great librarian blessed with a sponsored education, Cyril became a key player in the spread of education throughout the empire. He successfully added biblical studies "schools" to the existing centers of learning. For example, the lecturers at The Magnaura in Constantinople had excelled in Aristotelian and Platonic studies for hundreds of years. Cyril used his position to establish a "philosophy chair" there, which he for a time filled himself. This chair probably focused on what we would call "philosophy of religion," with an emphasis on knowledge of the biblical canon.

Though some historians anachronistically refer to such learning centers as "universities," they were very different from modern academic centers. Constantinople, Tarsus, and other eastern "schools" have very little in common with the university where I serve on faculty or any other contemporary college or university. Later medieval universities like Bologna, Paris, and Oxford in the West borrowed from the Eastern model and give us a better glimpse of how Cyril's work functioned in The Magnaura of Constantinople. A scholar such as Cyril established a "school," often with funding from church or state, and began enrolling students who moved to the city to learn. These schools were grouped as quasi-independent sections of the "university"—which became inextricably connected with the management of the city itself.

Cyril apparently was a very gifted linguist, mastering both Hebrew and Arabic. Leveraging those skills, the state sent him to improve relations between the Abbasid Caliphate and the Byzantine Empire. Though our sources are scanty, all agree that he chose the doctrine of the Trinity as his point of discussion. One cannot help but wonder whether this shows remarkable craftiness or foolishness. It may have been wise to face head on one of the most contentious points of disagreement between Islam and Christianity. However, it may also represent the overconfidence of a young scholar. We have no idea how the conference ended, but the two giant powers continued trade relations afterwards, so things must not have gone too badly.

Sometime in or near 860, the Roman (Byzantine) Emperor Michael III and Photios, Cyril's former teacher who had risen to become Patriarch of Constantinople,[6] asked Cyril to undertake another state-church mission. He was dispatched to the Khazars, a polyglot people group to the east. For about 300 years (660–960), the Khazar Khaganate dominated trade on the western Silk Road, their territory stretching from the Volga-Don steppes to the Crimea and the Caucasus Mountains. Maintaining their position was no small achievement considering the Khazars' powerful neighbors—the Abbasid Muslim Caliphate to their southwest, the Sasanian Persian Empire to their southeast, the semi-wild Rus to their north, and the Eastern Roman (Byzantine) Empire to their west.

Cyril's mission was vitally important for both ecclesiastical and economic reasons. Word had reached Constantinople that the Khagan (leader of the Khazar chieftains) was considering the wholesale imposition on his people of a somewhat bastardized form of Rabbinic Judaism. Previously, the people had followed a syncretized mix of shamanism, ancestor worship, animism, and polytheism known as Tengrism (or Tengerism). Some had converted to Christianity and some to Islam, but the base religion allowed for that diversity. With the adoption of Judaism, religious freedoms were being curtailed. Further, it was causing friction with the trade partners along the Silk Road.

Cyril was sent to debate and convince the Khagan of the superiority of Christianity. At the least, the emperor desired each Khazar tribe be allowed to choose their religion. Unsubstantiated legend claims that while en route through the Crimea, Cyril learned the challenging Khazar language. One questionable late-western source states that he was accompanied by his brother Methodius. Whoever came along, their presence made little difference, as the mission was an utter failure. Not only did the Khagan reject Cyril's arguments for the Bible and Christianity, he fully implemented his previous plan. All Khazars were forced into his syncretized Judaism.

This defeat must not have been viewed as any failing on Cyril's part, because the Emperor Michael III and Patriarch Photios soon after sent Cyril on another mission—one that would make a deep impact on the world. In 862, Rastislav, the second prince of Great Moravia, asked Constantinople for help in evangelizing his subjects. The Moravians were the first of the so-called "West Slavic" people to settle in Europe, and their kingdom covered the area roughly equivalent to modern Poland, Czech Republic, Slovakia, and Hungary.

This opportunity surely excited both emperor and patriarch, particularly in light of the icon controversy. Michael III and Photios were committed to icon proliferation. Educated by Photios, Cyril showed the same dedication. Great Moravia represented a great opportunity to expand the base of churches using icons. Just as important, this request from Moravia contained enormous political potential. Rastislav had come to his rule with the help of a western Frankish ruler named Louis the German. Nonetheless, he chafed under the western "support" of the Franks. To weaken their influence, he asked for missionaries to diminish the power of the Franks exercised through their Latin-speaking clergy.

One must not be deceived by the word "evangelize" in Ratislav's request. Later in the document he related to Michael III that his people had already turned from paganism to Christianity. In fact, he proudly declared that they lived according to Christian "law." Rastislav's desire was for Orthodox Christians from Constantinople to break the hold of Latin westerners on his country's culture and politics.

Michael III immediately sent Cyril and Methodius. The brothers set to work with great energy and efficiency. By 863 they had trained many assistants and formed what historians call the Great Moravian Academy. Fortified with disciples, they then embarked on a wildly ambitious project—translating church liturgy and even the Bible into a tongue the Slavic people could understand intuitively. To do so, they first needed to invent an alphabet. With almost superhuman speed, the brothers devised the Glagolitic alphabet. We don't know the original name for their novel invention, but centuries later it became known as Glagolitic. The appellation is quite appropriate, given that *glagol* (глаголъ) means "utterance."

The alphabet contained 41 letters, including many that were non-Greek sounds. A few exhibit remarkable creativity. For example, many scholars think the *sha* **Ш** and *tsi* **Ⱌ** letters of Glagolitic were based on the *shin* ש and *tsadi* צ letters in Hebrew.[7] Apparently, Cyril and Methodius took sounds known to them from their learning and adapted those sounds into new letters created to correspond to the sounds they heard from the Moravian Slavs. The language that evolved from the alphabet became known as Old Church Slavonic. That it was the creation of Cyril's team seems certain, attested by eastern and western sources alike. For example, a papal letter of 880 (*Industriae tuae*) declares that Old Church Slavonic was "invented by Constantine the Philosopher."

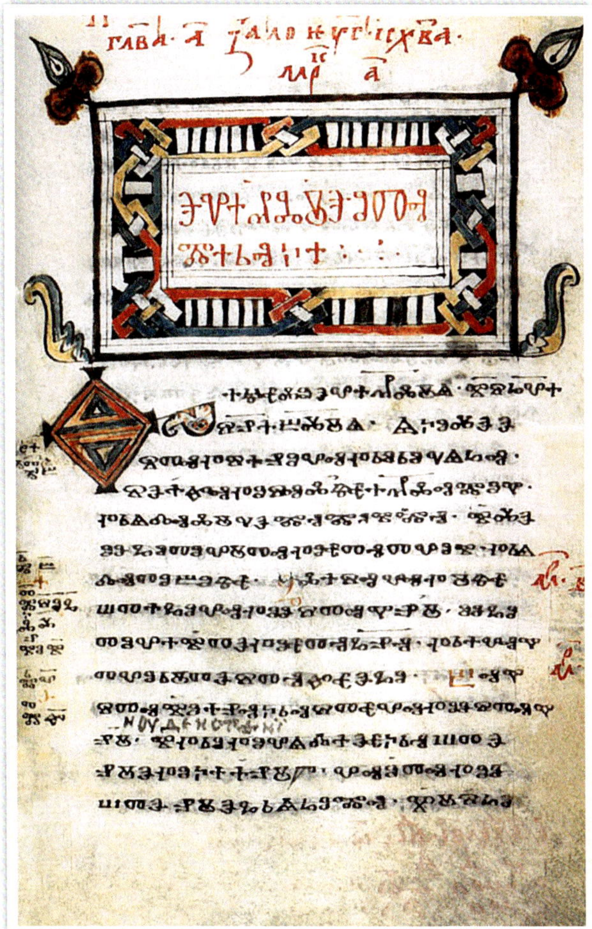

Glagolitic alphabet in Codex Zagrophensis, a late- 10th-early 11th-c. translation of the Gospels, Russian National Library Online Collection

To quickly wrap the language thread of the history, a number of Methodius' disciples continued to teach Old Church Slavonic, even after Cyril and Methodius went to Rome (about which more in a moment.) Some became very proficient educators, including Naum and Clement (of Ohrid, not to be confused with Clement of Rome 800 years his senior). Eventually, the Latin churches began to lash out against Old Church Slavonic, culminating in an AD 885 prohibition promulgated by a Frankish bishop named Wiching. The papacy approved the prohibition of Slavic worship, forcing Naum, Clement of Ohrid, and others to flee south into newly-Christianized Bulgaria. The Bulgarian tsar Boris I welcomed them as he feared the influence of Constantinople spread through worship conducted in Greek.

Methodius-trained scholars founded two great schools in Bulgaria. There, Clement taught a cumulative 3500 pupils Old Church Slavonic and Naum created a modified and simpler Slavic alphabet. He dubbed the new alphabet Cyrillic, in honor of the great Cyril. It became indispensable in the eventual conversion of the Rus, the creation of their language, the translation of the Bible into Russian, and the transfer of Orthodoxy's seat of power to Moscow after the fall of Constantinople in 1453.

Clearly, Cyril became one of the most influential thinkers in eastern European and western Asian history. Further, one cannot help but wonder how Cyril and Methodius's remarkable success contributed to the long-term thinking in Rome. While nothing can be directly connected, it was not too long after their successful work in Moravia that the papacy began to take a very dim view of any translation rendering scripture into common tongues. As Wycliffe and Tyndale would discover some 500 years later, translating the Bible to common languages became a sure means of inciting anger from the medieval Vatican.

The new language rapidly transformed Moravian society. People flocked to hear the liturgy performed in their own tongue. At first, the Latin priests seem to accept the situation with equanimity. Even our extant Slavic sources—which tend to be somewhat anti-Latin—note that the Frankish bishops applauded Methodius' rendering of the first Slavic Civil Code. This watershed creation established Moravian society on more biblical moral footing, or to use an anachronistic Enlightenment phrase, "set the civil law as a reflection of natural law." We also know of no serious opposition to Cyril's Bible translation. How much was actually translated is unknown, though the Gospels were written in Old Church Slavonic. It is debated whether the entire New Testament was rendered into Slavonic, but some Psalms and Old Testament sections were likely translated.

However, liturgy proved to be the serious point of contention. Some eastern historians pronounce that the Latin priests objected to the brothers popularizing liturgies from Constantinople instead of ones approved in Rome. Western sources tend to assert that it was language that caused difficulties. They say that the Frankish priests believed the Mass should only be celebrated in Latin. Regardless of the cause, the situation became so tense that Cyril and Methodius were compelled to travel to Rome in an effort to reach a solution.

The critical dispute is the source of that compulsion. Eastern Christians did not recognize the papacy as legitimately authoritative over all bishops, though they did recognize the Archbishop of Rome as an important ecclesiastical figure. Thus, eastern sources are somewhat emphatic in stressing the magnanimous nature of the brothers' choice to travel west. In this telling, Cyril was almost condescending, traveling as a duly-appointed legate of the emperor and the patriarch to reach a peaceful settlement of the controversy.

Not unexpectedly, western versions differ on this point. They contend that Pope Nicholas I (later St. Nicholas I) exerted papal authority to call the brothers to Rome. Nicholas was one of the early advocates for extended papal authority, even overruling a minor church council on his own initiative. Pope Nicholas was also no stranger to Byzantine ecclesiastical politics, as he had lobbied for the deposed Ignatios to be reestablished as patriarch of Constantinople instead of Photios. Western versions imply that the Slavic missionaries were more than happy to accede with Pope Nicholas' summons, and even stopped in the Crimea to get the bones of St. Clement in order to bring them home to Rome.

Whatever the source of the impetus to travel, and with or without St. Clement's bones, the brothers arrived in Rome in 868. Nicholas I had died by then, succeeded by Adrian II. Here again, the story paths diverge. Russian historians contend that Cyril and Methodius were duped by the aged Adrian II. Pope Adrian originally treated them well and issued a statement affirming the use of the Slavic language in church liturgy. However, he trapped the brothers in Rome, anticipating that within five years a papal prohibition against Slavic liturgy would be issued. While Cyril was touted as a genius, brilliant theologian, and wise philosopher, he was nonetheless confined to the Vatican libraries and not allowed to leave for Moravia. Methodius was likewise put to work and prohibited from leaving Rome.

Roman sources strongly disagree. They point to the approval of Slavic language liturgy by Adrian II and letters from important Romans such as Anastasius, praising Cyril's great knowledge. These same writers also insist that Methodius was ordained as a priest by the pope himself, even procuring *en abstentia* blessings for his disciples Clement of Ohrid and Naum. Some sources claim Cyril was also set aside as priest by Adrian II, having never before taken orders. The later *Translatio* record even claims that Cyril received a bishopric. It also contends that Adrian II gave him the name Cyril. Supposedly, he had gone by Constantine up to that point. The brothers are said to have remained voluntarily in Rome, where they were allowed to officiate and teach in Slavonic at the titular churches.

The plot thickens as one considers the events subsequently unfolding in the East. In 869, Adrian II asked for and sent legates to a major church council held in Constantinople (Fourth Council of Constantinople). The Emperor Basil I, murderer of and successor to Michael III, apparently agreed with the idea and jointly called for the council. Two issues were on the docket: 1) to permanently decide whether icons were allowed in worship as had been supported at the Second Council of Nicaea in 787, and 2) to depose Patriarch Photios.

After a few months, the council of bishops reached their conclusions. Icons were affirmed as valid. Further, they received exalted status, the official pronouncement declaring an icon of Christ *as important as* the written gospels. While the declaration of this council stopped short of saying that a person could find justification in revering an icon, it used the terms "so to..." in comparing icons to the salvation contained in the Scriptures. At the very least, looking at an image was deemed extremely profitable.

Patriarch Photios was removed, despite his unassailable status as an iconodule. We don't know precisely why Photios was forced out as patriarch. The most reasonable supposition concerns his elevation to the office. Remember that Empress Mother Theodora appointed Ignatios to succeed Methodios I. Ten years later, when Michael III removed his mother as regent, he also deposed Ignatios in favor of Photios. Since Ignatios had never received a proper trial required in canon law, Photios was deemed an imposter.

Some western sources also claim that Photios was teaching the heretical idea that redeemed humans possess dual souls—one perfect and the other still tainted by the flesh or sin nature. This is a scripturally untenable idea, but it is unclear whether Photios actually held it. Regardless, he was removed, pleasing papal supporters. For clarity's sake, it must be noted that the second of these decisions was overturned ten years later, after Patriarch Ignatios' death. A second Fourth Council of

Constantinople was held, which reinstated Photios. That gathering also dealt with the status of the Bulgarian churches and the *filioque* addition to the Nicene Creed.[8] For our purposes, the significant point is that the western church soon rejected the second council, despite the presence of papal legates who are reported to have agreed with the decisions. Likewise, the eastern church disavowed the first council, even though Emperor Basil and Patriarch Ignatios were signatories. Thus, if one should do an internet search of "Council of Constantinople IV," one will be forced to choose between the Roman Catholic/western version and the Orthodox/eastern version.

This was the spirit of the age in which Cyril and Methodius lived in Rome. Though the final split between western and eastern churches—known as the Great Schism—wouldn't be official until 1054, the Photian Schism reveals deep distrust rising between Rome and Constantinople.

Rediscovery of St. Cyril

When Father Mullooly began his excavations, witnesses were staggered by the massive volume of debris that was removed. The space revealed beneath San Clemente was immense. In order to support the 12th-century basilica above, the open space of the old church had been filled with tons of what can only be described as junk. Old bits of Roman stones, ancient paving, pottery pieces—anything that could fill the void was apparently thrown in to build up the base for the new construction.[9]

Important items were taken out of the 4th-century basilica before the back-filling process. For example, expensive columns were removed for reuse, and the relic bones purported to be those of St. Clement were taken out before dumping in back-fill. The bones were re-entombed with an anchor inside the high altar of the new church.

However, the debris pile below still contained a large sarcophagus that was bricked over. A mosaic icon declared this to be the final resting place of St.Cyril. Clearly, this tomb was *not* transported above to become part of the new construction. When I first visited San Clemente, the original finding had remained in stasis since Father Mullooly's discovery in the 1850s.

This discovery leant weight to the long-standing Russian contention that St. Cyril was unappreciated and trapped in Rome. While all agree that St. Cyril died in Rome in early 870[10]—after which Methodius returned to the East—supposedly by the 12th century no one could remember where he was buried. If indeed St. Cyril was appreciated and even venerated in Rome, it seems unbelievable that when construction began on the 12th-century basilica his bones would have been left below it.

In contrast, some Latin records proclaim that St. Cyril was so popular in Rome that the people clamored for his body to be buried in the city when he died. According to these accounts, Methodius allowed the Romans to keep the body because Adrian II was so fond of him and because the people immediately called for Cyril to be canonized. This also seems slanted and unlikely.

The high altar of the Basilica di San Clemente, begun in the 12th c.
What are believed to be the bones of the 1st-century Church Father Clement
are entombed in the red marble sarcophagus beneath the marble canopy.

Saint John Paul II prays before the tomb of St. Cyril on December 31, 1980. Earlier that day he issued an encyclical praising St. Cyril and St. Methodius [Egregiae virtutis]. *Photo L'Osservatore Romano January 1, 1981.*

The truth probably lies in some combination of accounts that unfortunately cannot be fully discerned at this juncture. Cyril probably was appreciated in Rome, an understandable reaction to the greatest scholar of his day. Yet, there is something questionable about the fact that Cyril never left Rome, especially given the charged atmosphere surrounding the *filioque* controversy, Photian Schism, and arguments regarding vernacular preaching. Add to those the ill feelings engendered by the Great Schism just before construction began on the new basilica, and it seems possible that whatever his reception in 9th-century Rome, St. Cyril's remains were purposefully left in the 12th-century pile of debris.

St. Cyril's relics have continued to promote intrigue, especially once Slavic nationalism blossomed after the First World War. The Vatican issued a statement under Pope Paul VI (r. 1963–1978) that the relics of St. Cyril had never actually been buried under rubble. Rather, he said, they were hidden during the French Revolution and sadly, misplaced. Pope Paul VI subsequently found one of the bones and had it reinterred at

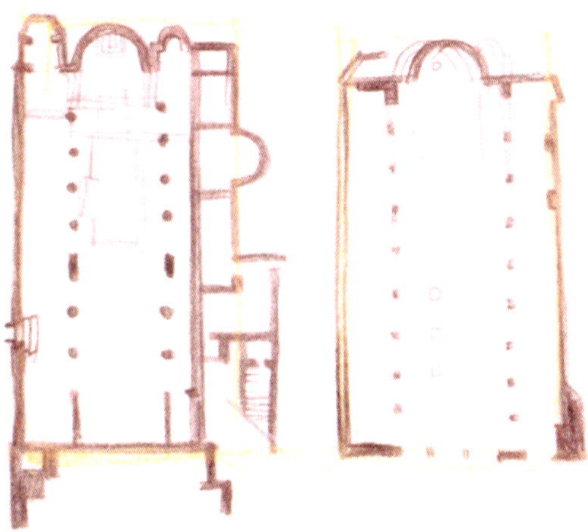

The sketch represents a rough plan of the upper basilica (left) and the church beneath. (right). Sketch by Christen McClure

the 4th-century church site under the icon of St. Cyril. A talented archaeologist employed by the Vatican—who shall remain nameless—told me, "The proclamation of Paul VI did more harm than good in relations between the Holy See and countries behind the Iron Curtain."

In 2016, Pope Francis met at the Havana, Cuba airport with Patriarch Kirill of Moscow. Their politically-charged photo-opportunity and discussion dominated the news coverage, burying what may have been the most lasting aspect of the meeting. Pope Francis gave the Orthodox Church a reliquary containing a bone of St. Cyril, a move designed to thaw relations. Thus, whatever the reality of St. Clement's bones going west, St. Cyril's bone has finally made a long trip back east.

The Church Below

Of course, St. Cyril's tomb is not the only interesting thing uncovered in the basilica by Fr. Mullooly and di Rossi. Though other sources do an excellent job detailing the important aspects of the basilica used from the 4th–11th centuries, a few things relate to our theme of East-West relations and should receive comment here.

Wall remains

Descending the stairs and looking to the left (east), one sees the limit of reclamation. The wall there is a fascinating mix of original construction and compacted debris. The far north and south parts of this eastern wall are original construction covering the 4th-century narthex. A few feet up the north side, one can see di Rossi's reconstruction of the original dedication inscription, pieced together from the broken cornerstone. The center is choked and was an amalgamation of debris, giving a good feel for the challenges faced by the original excavators.

This area is the narthex of the lower church. Further east would have been the open atrium surrounded by a colonnade, as can be seen in the diagram of the plan of the lower church found on page 58.

The Particular Judgment

Facing about in the middle of the narthex, one is struck by a badly damaged fresco. Using X-ray imaging, art historians have convincingly recreated the scene and titled it *The Particular Judgment*. In St. Paul's epistles *1 Corinthians* 3 and *2 Corinthians* 5, he describes the *bema*, or "judgment seat" of Christ. This is the adjudication wherein Christians will receive rewards or face loss of reward and is separate from the Great White Throne judgement of non-believers detailed in *Revelation* 20.

Over the first Christian millennium, these two judgments became conflated and have remained blurred in both Roman and Orthodox theology, though they are separate events in most Protestant theology.[11] This fresco represents a transitional period where the views were blending, yet the judgments had not yet fully combined.

The Particular Judgment, *artist unknown*

The Particular Judgment, *after cleaning and restoration*

On the fresco, Jesus is judging two Christians, almost certainly St. Cyril and St. Methodius. Cyril is on the right, where Clement of Rome is testifying about him. The assessment shows no limbo or other signs of being a judgment for entrance to heaven; therefore, it is very likely Jesus is discerning the rewards He will bestow on the brothers.

Next to Clement is the Archangel Michael, the great warrior of heaven. On the left, St. Methodius kneels as Andrew the Apostle speaks on his behalf. This is a nod to early legend that Andrew also evangelized the Slavs. The angel Gabriel—seen throughout the Bible as bringer of news about Messiah—is next to St. Andrew.

The fresco must have been commissioned after 885 when Methodius died. It shows the high regard for the "Apostles to the Slavs" among the Roman Christians. It strikes one as odd that this large fresco blocks the entrance from the narthex into the church; however, the large doorway was arched and bricked over to add stability after the earthquake of 847. When the church entrance had to be bricked for safety, *The Particular Judgment* fresco served as a stunning wall covering in the Byzantine style. Modern restoration experts have reconditioned the fresco and today one can see their updated version of *The Particular Judgment*. It gives a good sense of the vibrancy of the original art before the site was filled in.

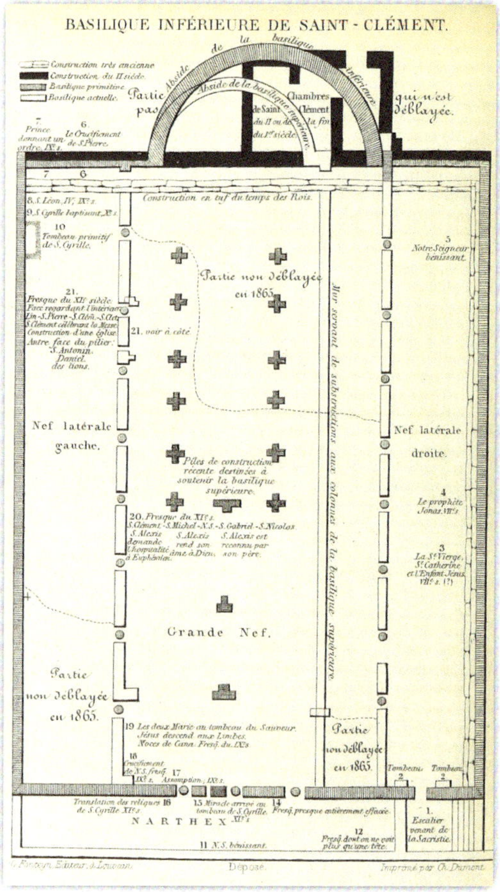

Image from: Rome et ses monuments. Guide du voyageur catholique dans la capitale du monde chrétien Avec cinquante-et-un plans annotés by Édouard Philippe Jacques de Blesser, p. 280, 1866.

The baptistery

Turning about and heading back toward the stairs (north), one is forced to curve left (west) into the north aisle. This north aisle was the scene of Fr. Mullooly's breakthrough. The first and most controversial discovery is a sizeable room behind a perpetually-locked iron grate. Perhaps the importance and impact of this gated space can be appreciated best through my own experience in 2012:

> A Vatican expert walked me down to the lower church.[12] Using a large, old-fashioned key, he unlocked the forbidden gate. We stooped to fit through the opening and travelled along a small hallway running northward. Suddenly, the hallway opened to reveal a room roughly of 60 square meters (800 sq. ft.). There, the archaeologist pointed to a round concrete receptacle in the floor—a structure almost a meter deep with a diameter of around two meters. He then began his interrogatory lesson:
>
> Archaeologist: And what do you suppose that might be, Mister Dr. of Bible?
>
> Wayne: If I didn't know better, I would say that was a baptistery.
>
> A: And why would you say you know better? What do you think you know about early medieval baptism?

Baptistery in the lowest level of St. Demtrios, Thessaloniki
(Photographs of the San Clemente baptistery are prohibited.)

W: Frankly, I know little. I would assume that it was done via sprinkling, in which case this large amount of water would seem odd.

A: Aye, it would. And that's because this was indeed a baptistery, but they weren't doing any sprinkling in these waters. This was for immersion.

W: Wow!

A: Now, how late do you think this structure is?

W: The absence of marble would cause me to lean toward 5th c. or later.

A: Spot on! Had it been part of the original 4th c. construction, it would almost certainly have been made of marble. Now, what is that niche over there for?

W: I hadn't noticed it. Since it is cut into the wall directly opposite the baptistery and isn't very large, I would assume it was made for an observer.

A: Correct! It was most likely used by the bishop of Rome or later by cardinals connected to this basilica. They would bless the proceedings as a priest climbed in and immersed the new Christian in baptism.

W: I must ask...

A: (Interrupting) Before you ask, I know your question. No, they weren't dunking any babies down here! This is one of a number of sites that argue that immersion was the most widespread form of baptism in the earliest churches and that it was performed on believers, not infants. It also explains why my superiors up the hill (he gestured toward street level in the direction of the Vatican hill) keep this door locked. It helps to prevent uncomfortable questions.

W: I have seen a similar structure in Thessaloniki at the level of the earliest church. Same purpose?

A: Aye. And I have found similar baptisteries in Syria and Iran, though I have to steal across the borders to get to them. There are brilliant and ancient churches there that are rotting from neglect. I sneak in over the hills and record the details while something still can be seen.

The Universal Judgment

Emerging from the baptistery and turning right (west) down the north aisle, one is confronted with a remarkable painting. Known today as *The Universal Judgment,* this fresco is dated to around 885, not long after the death of St. Cyril. The characters in the fresco cannot be identified with certainty. However, the saints standing with Jesus at the judgment are from many

The Universal Judgment, *artist unknown*

different people groups. Both eastern and western Christians are depicted with varying facial structure, hair, bearding, and clothing. This may speak to a remaining unity of understanding even after the Photian Schism of 863–867.

Empress fresco

In a niche on the right is a fresco of Madonna and Child, or so it appears as first glance. Actually, this painting was originally made to honor the Arian Empress Theodora of the [Byzantine] Roman empire. From Constantinople, she and her husband, the energetic Emperor Justinian, sent a great deal of money west in 533. These funds were used to refinish churches in Rome, to spread Justinian's recodification of Roman law, and to re-establish civilized Roman rule in Italy. The first two goals met with lasting success, but the third did not.

Most art historians assume that Theodora, who died in 548, was standing in the original depiction and possibly holding a donative box of gold for the church. Sadly, we cannot see her right hand, which was raised in blessing. It would be interesting to know whether her hand was offering the Orthodox style of blessing.[13] Sometime later, the painting was heavily retouched. The woman was seated and a Christ child placed in her lap. Her arm was elongated to a grotesque proportion in order to accommodate the Child. Most historians reason that this transformation reflected dissatisfaction with the church in Constantinople.

From this north aisle, one can go south into the nave (central aspect) of the church. There are only two entrances today from

The Empress Fresco *commissioned by the Rapiza family, artist unknown*

the north aisle into the nave, because of buttressing necessary to hold up the basilica above as the rubble was removed.

The far eastern side of the nave once opened to the narthex, but as noted above, the earthquake of 847 necessitated blocking up the space. On the narthex side one finds *The Particular Judgment*. On the nave side are a series of paintings paid for by

The Miracle of the Black Sea,
artist unknown

Beno de Rapiza and his wife, Maris Marcellaria, whose names are recorded in the plaster along with those of their children, Clement and Altilia. Two of those frescoes relate to this chapter—*The Miracle of the Black Sea* and *The Transfer of the Remains of St. Clement.*

Earlier in the book, we referenced the legend of a child miraculously saved when his drowned body touched the divinely-built tomb of St. Clement. That story is interpreted in the 11th-century artwork known as *The Miracle of the Black Sea.* The top panel shows the child revived by the canopied tomb under the waters and being reunited with his mother as his village cheers. The medallion in the middle represents St. Clement, with the Rapiza family below. The legend to the right preserves the information.

The second fresco of interest is *The Transfer of the Remains of St. Clement.* In the painting, the 11th-century understanding of a 9th-century event is revealed. The people and a large number of priests are rejoicing as the body of St. Clement, miraculously

The Transfer of the Remains of St. Clement, *artist unknown*

recovered by Cyril, is brought to the basilica. Actually, the picture indicates that this is a transfer of St. Clement's relics from St. Peter's Basilica to San Clemente. Methodius and Cyril are to the left on either side of the pope. The artist mistakenly identified the pope as Nicholas, but Adrian II was on the throne by the time the brothers arrived from the East.

The nave also contains many fine frescoes from the 9th century or earlier. These are found on both north and south walls and mainly cover biblical scenes. On the south wall near the altar (to the west), one finds a final depiction that speaks to this place where medieval East and West seem to comingle. The fresco—near the doorway to the south aisle and the tomb of St. Cyril—is yet another endowment by the Rapiza family.

The top section was cut off when the upper basilica was constructed, but originally showed Clement standing with the Apostle Peter and the other early bishops of Rome. This was influenced by the campaign to grow the strength of the papacy in the years after Pope Innocent III. The assumption was that an unbroken line of apostolic succession granted the papacy more authority.

Somewhat ironically, rest of the fresco concerns a Greek legend of one Sisinnius. Although no eastern Christian would have accepted perceived propaganda for apostolic Roman succession, they would have recognized immediately the Sisinnius story. Historian Guy Bedouelle summarizes: "The fresco...recalls the punishment of the pagan Sisinius [sic], who became blind after trying to force his wife Theodora, who was a Christian, to leave the Church."[14]

The Legend of Sisinnius, artist unknown

No reputable ancient sources mention Sisinnius, but later Greek hagiography has many versions of the legend shown in the basilica. The inclusion of it in a piece made during the tensions of the Great Schism is thought-provoking. Were the priors of San Clemente (along with the family Rapiza and the artists) trying to show some form of East-West unity?

Although we don't understand the reasoning behind it, the painting itself is fairly straightforward. St. Clement has just begun to pray at church, an action often represented in art by raised hands. Theodora, a Christian woman near St. Clement's left hand and dressed in yellow, is surprised by her jealous husband, Sisinnius, who breaks into the service with his servant. Interestingly, the service does not appear to be in a basilica but rather a *domus ecclesia* (house church)—the villas of wealthy Romans used for 1st- and 2nd-century worship. As St. Clement is praying, Sisinnius and the servant are struck blind and deaf.

A word on location of the event is in order. In most instances, the legend takes place in the eastern Mediterranean, usually in the Cappadocian region of the Eastern Empire (modern eastern Turkey and northwestern Syria). How Clement came to be there is not explained and it is a good distance from the Crimea where other legends have him banished. In a few versions, this miracle occurs in Italy and Sisinnius is both a senator and a close friend of the Emperor Trajan. In that case, how his wife came to have a name that is clearly Greek is not revealed. Regardless, another layer of East-West combination is inherent in the narratives.

With respect to narrative, the bottom panel shows the ensuing scene at Sisinnius' villa. At Theodora's urging, Clement went to their home and prayed for the men, who were immediately healed. However, Sisinnius assumed that this was sorcery, and called for his servants to seize Clement. The attackers were confounded by God, mistaking the heavy columns of a building project for their target. The servant and Sisinnius are yelling, and the inscriptions of their speech contain the earliest examples of vernacular Italian in art. Sisinnius, to the far right of the panel, screams, "FILI DELE PUTE TRAITE" ["Pull, you

Central part of the 4th-century nave, photo by Janna Braudrick

sons of whores!"] and the servant shouts, "FALITE DERETO COLO PALO" ["Get behind with a pole!"]. One assumes that the servant is talking to the other servants and not his master, imploring them to use a lever to lift the marble pillar which he assumed to be the dead-weight of a limp Clement. The Italian is another puzzling part of this fresco. While all the rest has been astonishingly close to 1st-century reality, this vernacular is very 11th century. Sisinnius' cry is also infamous as the first cursing written on a church wall.

In more refined and educated Latin, Clement replies to them, "DURITIAM CORDIS SAXA TRAERE MERUISTIS" ["You deserve to pull stones (because) your hearts are hard."] Though not shown in the fresco, apocryphal works go on to declare that Clement then led Sisinnius and hundreds of others to trust Jesus as Savior. Some commentators say this explains Trajan's ire toward St. Clement as a disturber of the peace.

The final fresco to observe on this level is the *Anastasis,* found near the southwest corner, just east of the sarcophagus of St. Cyril. Early in the 21st century, this work was painstakingly and beautifully restored through the work of Rome's Istituto Centrale per il Restauro.

Romans term this fresco "The Descent of Christ into Limbo." It describes what the Orthodox Church calls the "Anastasis," and early Lutherans described as "The Harrowing of Hell." It was the last fresco discovered by Fr. Mullooly.

The official website for Basilica di San Clemente describes the work:

The Anastasis. *Artist unknown, photo © Holy See*

The fresco depicts the Lord Jesus Christ after his death, surrounded by glory and bearing his Cross like a standard, descending into the Underworld to rescue the souls of those who had died before his coming. He treads on a demon who, amid the tongues of flame, has taken hold of Adam's foot. The scene celebrates the Lord's victory over the bonds of death and the power of the devil.

To the left and separated from the main scene by a spiral column there is a painting of a figure carrying a Book

> of the Gospels. His beard and decorated hood indicate that he is an Eastern monk. The fresco appears to have been part of the funeral monument of this monk who was buried here. The position and character of the tomb, corresponding as it does with contemporary accounts of his funeral in the Basilica di San Clemente, has recently led scholars to propose that this is the original tomb and portrait of St Cyril, the Apostle of the Slavs.[15]

Meanwhile, more reliable information regarding St. Clement can be found in the lowest level of the building just beneath the *Clement and Sisinnius* fresco.

CHAPTER 3

SAN CLEMENTE'S FLOODS AND FURNITURE

When de Rossi and Fr. Mullooly cleared the 4th-century basilica, they also found a deeper gap under the far western part of the basilica. They discovered a narrow brick alley between two buildings. In fact, the original walls of those buildings were major supports holding up both basilicas above them.

Alley space between the two 1st-century buildings

To the west, the bricks appeared similar to those used in apartments built during the period from the 2nd century BC to the 2nd century AD. The tufa blocks of the eastern wall were likely from a more industrial construction, though of the same period. In Fr. Mullooly's phrase, the area contained "quite a bit" of water, and they were limited in examining much further. They did notice that the apartment building was obviously separate and in no way connected with the church building across the alley. Further, some small rooms of the apartment building contained objects associated with the worship of the Roman mystery god Mithras, not Jesus Christ.

Mithraic Worship and Instruction

Mithraism is one of the religions about which we know just enough to be frustrated by our lack of information. It likely began in Persia as a pre-Zoroastrian sect, and is still a religious tradition among some Zoroastrians to this day. As it came to Rome, Mithraism morphed dramatically. Instead of leading a theistic belief system, Mithras the god became purveyor of a mystery religion. This makes Mithraism as it came to Rome much more akin to the Eleusinian Mysteries of Greece than the Mithraism practiced in Persia.

The Mithraic Mysteries became popular in the Roman military, especially in the western empire from the late 1st through the early 4th centuries. The worshippers went through seven grades of initiation based on knowledge and repetition. Like all mystery religions, it was forbidden to speak of the process of initiation, making the modern historian's task very difficult. One can assume they shared a secret handshake, given that initiates referred to themselves as *syndexioi*—"ones united in the handshake."

In both his letters to the Romans and the Colossians in the New Testament, the Apostle Paul makes a strong delineation between mystery religions and Christianity, something to be examined in the final chapter. The real mystery is not whether Mithraism influenced Christianity. As St. Paul shows definitively, the worldviews are utterly separate and opposed. The mystery concerns why a mithraeum ever existed on this site. The discovery is astonishing—not because of anything connected to Christianity, but due to Mithraic worship itself.

Adherants of Mitrhaism met in temples housed underground with openings above—a necessary part of the bull sacrifice ceremony in which the initiate was bathed with blood from above. Dozens of these mithraea have been found around Rome, quite a few near the Flavian Amphitheatre (Colosseum) and the gladiatorial barracks, structures which are mere steps away from Basilica di San Clemente.

This requirement to worship underground sparks yet another mystery connected to San Clemente. Were the *syndexioi* on this site the only ones to worship above ground? Did they own the second-story apartments above, cutting a hole through the floor to allow for the sacrificial blood to spill into their triclinium?

The triclinium of the Mithraeum, photo by Janna Braudrick

Or, did they come to the site in the 4th century, when the neighborhood was silting up? By that point, construction had begun on Basilica di San Clemente which sat at the new street level more than ten feet above and extended over both the apartment building and the existing church space. If so, the timing is unexpected, given that Mithraism disappears from the empire within a few decades of the Emperor Constantine's Edict of Milan in 313. In fact, there is no trace of western Mithraism by the end of the 4th century.[16]

Although the solution remains unknown, it is a fact that Fr. Mullooly discovered a Mithraeum under the far western end of the basilica. The most reasonable scenario is that this was a late Mithraeum that was only used for a short season before the cult died out.

Great flood and great wars

In 1911, Rome suffered from a ruinous flood—one of many through the centuries. The waters in the Mithraeum rose to such a level that they threatened the art in the 4th-century basilica. In response, Father Louis Nolan of San Clemente dug a relief channel, correctly reasoning that an ancient sluice toward the Tiber River must exist underneath. His actions became metaphorical for the deepened investigation into the site. No resurrection-providing

Piazza Navona during the flood of 1870
Photo public domain

tombs were uncovered under the waters, but historical finds of great significance were discovered.

This propensity of Rome to flood offers another explanation why the city street level kept rising through the years when Rome was less populated. Sometimes it proves easier to rebuild on top of alluvial and debris deposits after a flood than to dig out from the flood damage. As a comparison, Florence was devastated by a flood in 1966 that deposited an estimated 600,000 tons of mud on the city. Even with modern equipment, digging out was a long and tedious endeavor.

As what Fr. Nolan called "the lake" drained from the apartments and the alleyway, he observed that the Mithraic complex had more than merely a triclinium. A number of rooms appeared to have been set aside solely for use in the mystery religion. Most

The Mithraic school

astounding was the discovery of the "Mithraic school." This room represents the educational heart of the mystery religion. Around the walls, one can see the seven simple Roman numerals that delineate the instruction or seating areas for each level of *syndexioi*.[17]

Due to the depredations of The Great War (1914–1918), excavations were halted. In 1937, Father Pius O'Daly took a radical approach to renewed inquiry. Following the tradition that St. Clement had actually taught on this site, O'Daly broke through the tufa wall across the alley from the apartments. He hoped to find an ancient basilica beyond the stones and was not disappointed. The exact nature of the structure is debated, but it seemed very likely that it was large and important. Father O'Daly triumphantly claimed that he had found the original basilica

The lowest level, where Fr. O'Daly broke through

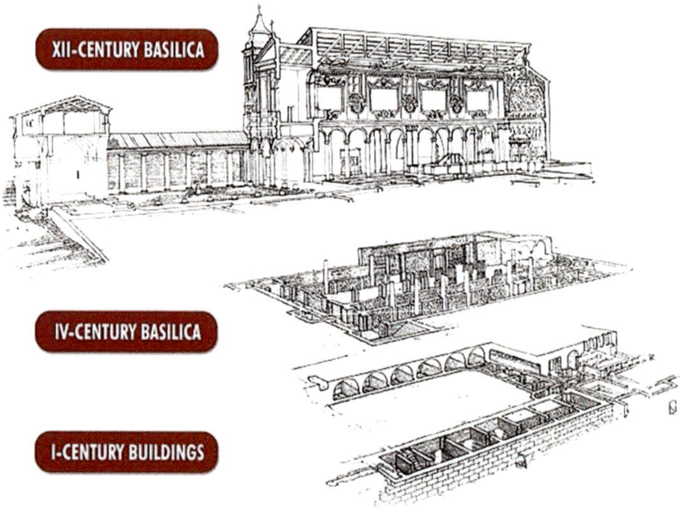

Vatican reconstruction of the layers at the site, © Holy See

used by the 1st-century church. However, the Second World War interrupted full excavation. As the fighting in Italy concluded in 1945, Father Raymond Dowdall extended the diggings of the 1st-century space to roughly where they are today.

The provenance of this very large space is a source of much contention, and sadly, little of it has been unearthed. It again shows signs of having been filled with junk in order to support the construction above it. However, the tufa block walls and interior brick structures are quite strong. In fact, they represent a tidier and more expensive kind of construction that what one sees in the 4th-century building. And a spring of living water flows in the southwest corner of the building as was mentioned in the prologue.[18]

Titus Flavius Clemens (d. AD 95)

Father Dowdall's assumption was that this space represented the home of Titus Flavius Clemens. Clemens was a member of the imperial family who was beheaded by his cousin, the Emperor Domitian (r. 81–96), reportedly in retaliation for Clemens's support of Christianity. There are three important factors to remember when considering such early persecution of Christians:

1. Christianity was considered a serious threat by the imperial structure. Because Christians refused to treat with any other possibility of deity, they were viewed as covertly, if not overtly, seditious. Of paramount importance to Romans was the stability of the empire, plagued as it had been by 200 years of periodic civil war. Thus, it is understandable that imperial officers feared Christians as a potential fifth column subverting society. Those familiar with the New Testament will find this difficult to accept, given the high value the Bible places on both work ethic and civil obedience. In fact, the New Testament presents anti-Christian agitators as the primary threats to civil order. Jews who

reject Jesus as Messiah stir up trouble while Roman government forces are more neutral. Nonetheless, by the end of the 1st century, Imperial Rome had become suspicious of Christians in degrees that varied according to location in the empire and local governance.

2. As already mentioned, Sir William Ramsay effectively uncovered that the church in the first two centuries grew most rapidly among the upper classes. Investigating the reasons for that is beyond the scope of this book. Nonetheless, the high society attraction to Jesus makes the possibility of sedition all the more threatening. Senators and equites have the financial wherewithal to topple an emperor, so their conversion to Jesus Christ is noteworthy.[19]

3. The Apostle Paul states that by the end of his ministry, the elite Praetorian Guard had been widely exposed to the gospel of Jesus, with many soldiers seemingly becoming Christians.[20] In his book *Praetorian,* Guy de la Bédoyère points out that the late 1st-century Praetorian Guard was not yet the king-making force it would become; however, it was surely troubling to see the Christian gospel take root in such an important force.

Each of these factors almost certainly played a role in the martyrdom of Titus Flavius Clemens, as did the temper of his cousin, the Emperor Domitian. Sources from the first and second centuries depict Domitian as an untrustworthy wretch. These writers are admittedly anti-Domitian, yet there is merit in their accusations. Christianity suffered greatly under Domitian, who was the first to enact wholesale legal marginalization and intense persecution of Christians.

The Clementine building

In such an environment, Clemens stands out as exceptionally bold. In fact, for centuries legend maintained that Clemens was so audacious that he allowed one of the Roman churches to meet in his own house. As a Flavian, it is certain that Clemens was a man of means and surely inhabited a large *domus*. Over many centuries these great villas were constructed according to a fairly regular plan. A dominant central space was available for gatherings. *Acts* 12 describes such a gathering in the home of Mary, a Jewish Roman citizen living in Jerusalem.

It is very possible that Titus Flavius Clemens had a large church gathering in his home. Called a *domus ecclesia,* such a house church was the normal setting for a 1st- or 2nd-century Christian church.

However, there is a serious problem with identifying the 1st-century site uncovered by Dowdall as a home. There are no windows! This would be unprecedented and unthinkable in the stifling humidity of Rome. Some archaeologists maintain that these were bricked over later, after Clemens' martyrdom. Although this is possible because the site was used as a church, the few walls we can access show no signs of window spaces bricked over and closed.

A more likely option is that this was a public building to which a Flavian would have had access. This would not be unusual, as classical buildings tended to serve multiple tenants. For example, the various *fora* in central Rome served as both centers of commerce and places of law. This is not restricted to the Romans. Ancient people conducted multiple aspects of business and public life in the "gates" of their settlements. Even large cities such as Megiddo in Israel boasted wide, niched gates to host a variety of legal, religious, political, and economic activities.

Father Paul Lawlor, archaeological researcher for the Vatican and 21st-century priest at St. Clement's, is convinced that this site was not a home at all. He reasons that this was indeed a public building, most likely an imperial mint. The possibility is intriguing. According to an inscription from the time of Hadrian (r. 118–138), Domitian moved an imperial mint from the *Arx*—a citadel on the Capitoline Hill. This relocation of this mint has never been determined, and it may be the site where Titus Flavius Clemens allowed a church to gather. Unless the remainder of the space is successfully excavated, the question cannot be answered with certainty. The space currently exposed is large enough to house a significant *domus ecclesia,* but is much too small for a mint. That said, it seems clear the building goes on eastward beyond the current exposure. What is seen now may be merely the public rooms of the mint, where exchange business happened on certain days.

A noteworthy aspect of the 1st-century structure is its lack of adornment. This would be understandable in a *domus ecclesia* or a public building. Yet in a building used exclusively or primarily for church, it strikes some as unusual that there are no frescoes. In fact, there was no altar uncovered at that level, despite meticulous sifting through the debris used to fill the space.[21] It is very unlikely that the church did not eventually occupy and own the space on a permanent basis. Conservative estimates include the late-3rd and 4th centuries for church occupation; others estimate an almost unbroken ecclesiastical usage from Clemens—who died in AD 95—until the start of the basilica above in the late 300s.

Perhaps the best explanation for the lack of decoration is that Christians in the first centuries practiced worship in styles very different from medieval forms. I have spent considerable time in early church buildings in Italy, Israel, Jordan, Turkey, and Greece. Friends (nameless for their protection) have researched similar sites in Syria and Lebanon. Together we concur that the earliest attestations of Christian worship largely were unadorned. Mosaic tiles appear to be the first kind of decoration used in churches, yet even mosaic floors did not become widespread until the 3rd century. These depict everything from mosaic patterns to the names of capital campaign donors. Altars are rare. Frescoes, which appear often in burial spaces, are very difficult to find in early worship spaces.

Regarding the activities of church worship, it would appear that our earliest witnesses are correct in reporting the centrality of scripture reading and preaching. St. Paul's epistle *1 Corinthians* and extra-biblical sources describe in some detail the Christian *agape* feast (agape is a Greek word for "love"). In large churches, this seems to have occurred in various small groups meeting in people's homes. In smaller churches, the whole church met in one villa. There, a large meal was held either as part of the celebration of the Lord's Supper/Holy Communion or as a precursor to it.

There is great debate regarding how often the early churches celebrated the *agape* feast. It was clearly an entrenched ordinance in worship by the mid-1st century. Yet, we cannot ascertain with certainty how often it was practiced. There are three valid options:

1. Some early Christians seem to have understood the *agape* meal [later termed Eucharist, Communion, Holy Communion, or Lord's Supper] as an activity to be practiced once a year. Jesus's command to take bread and cup in remembrance of Him was understood as an extension of the Jewish seder/Passover meal that He took with His disciples in *John* 13–17. While such may have been the observance in some places, it does not fit what we read from St. Paul regarding the abuses of hospitality at the Corinthian *agape* feasts.

2. Others understand the phrase "when you gather" in *1 Corinthians* 11:33 as calling for weekly observance. They held an *agape* feast on the first day of each week immediately after the church assembly. This later

became widespread as part of the observance of the Mass inside the churches and was ultimately adopted as official practice by the medieval Roman church. This is possibly the background in *1 Corinthians,* given the repetitive nature inherent in St. Paul's verbiage.

3. Many churches appear to have assumed that "when you gather" signified the regular feast meals that were part of classical life. Such meals were a significant aspect of Jewish and Greek communities. For Greek "clubs" this came about once a month, a time frame that also fits with St. Paul's epistle of *1 Corinthians.*

Comprehending the *agape* feast is important for understanding the simplicity of the San Clemente church site. It is also helpful for comparison with the Mithraic practices discussed in our last chapter.

Clement as a name

Sometimes it is confusing to understand how popular names of other eras bear such close resemblance to each other. Such is true with the name "Clement." We should not be surprised that a Clement is associated with a site opened to the church by a Clemens.[22] St. Clement will be the subject of the next chapter, but because he is connected to the 1st-century site, a brief discussion of the known facts about him is in order.

St. Paul mentions Clement by name in his letter to Philippi (*Philippians* 4:3). Most scholars reason that St. Paul was in his first Roman imprisonment at the time, dating the Philippian letter sometime in AD 61–62. It is quite likely that St. Clement was a young church leader at the time, and there is no solid reason to doubt the tradition that Clement led the church on the Clemens site. Clement was still pastoring in Rome when he authored an epistle of his own (known as *1 Clement*). Sent to the church in Corinth, the letter instructs the Corinthians on a series of issues, not least of which is obedience to their local church elders.[23]

St. Clement's letter is one of the earliest extant Christians writings outside of the New Testament. This letter is traditionally dated around AD 95–96. More liberal scholars assign it a later date, closer to the 2nd-century writer Hermas, who references Clement in his work *Shepherd*. Others believe that the reference to the Jerusalem temple in Clement 41:2 is evidence that the epistle was penned before AD 70. Based upon the writing style, it is thought that Clement was a freed Hebrew slave educated in Greek. His epistle displays a strong basis in the Old Testament and his quotations come from the Hebrew text rendered by him into Greek—as opposed to direct quotes from the Greek translation of the Old Testament known as the *Septuagint*. Additionally, Clement shows an understanding of slavery and sympathy toward the enslaved.

The presence of a Roman name such as "Clement" does not preclude the possibility of either Jewish ancestry or a slave background. There are many examples of military members who adopted popular Roman names such as "Clement." St. Clement's contemporary, historian Titus Flavius Josephus, was born Josef ben Matityahu (37–c. 100). His life shows that one could move from Hebrew slavery to a place of cultural importance where people address the former slave exclusively by the new Roman cognomen.

Clement emphasized the local leadership (presbyters or elders) in the church. Later writers bestow the title of "pope" upon him.[24] Tertullian (ca. 155–220) lists St. Clement as the second pope, and St. Jerome (ca. 342–420) lists him as the fourth (after St. Peter). St. Augustine (354–430) puts him second, while most other witnesses list him fourth. The confusion about St. Clement's position continued through Middle Ages and into the modern era. A telling example was recorded about 1450, when an unknown English speaker wrote a travelogue about his pilgrimage to Rome. Known as *A Solace of Pilgrims*, it contains this passage: "Of this same pope (seint clement) wil we telle you sum thingis which are in a doute a mongis many men. For summe sey that he was pope next petir and summe say that too were be for him."

Regardless of uncertainties and differences regarding details of St. Clement's life, there is no question that his work and writing were extremely influential in shaping the church in the early centuries of Christianity. No one should underestimate his importance then and now.

CHAPTER 4

ST. CLEMENT AND ST. PAUL

Leaving history and turning to the New Testament for a moment, consider further mysteries that arise from the Apostle Paul's *Epistle to the Romans:*

1. *Romans* focuses a lot of attention on the idea of slavery. The concept of slavery is referenced 11 times—more than in any other New Testament epistle. Why?

2. Why so much discussion of Judaism to a mixed Jew/Gentile church? In trying to reason through this interpolation into the text, New Testament scholar Everett F. Harrison states, "There remains, however, the awkward fact that the apostle devotes three whole chapters (9–11) to the nation of Israel."[25] No commentator seems to have definitive answers, and most admit that Rome seems an odd audience for that subject. Some even call chapters 9–11 an "awkward insertion," given that the end of chapter 8 flows quite nicely into the practical address that begins chapter 12.

Basilica di San Clemente, photo by Janna Braudrick

3. Why no mention of St. Clement? We know from *Philippians* (4:3) that Clement likely was a compatriot of St. Paul's during Paul's house arrest in Rome. Of course, *Romans* was written before St. Paul's arrival in the capital. Nonetheless, based on Paul's good intelligence system evident in *Romans* 16, it seems likely that the apostle should have known that Clement led one of the churches in Rome. The simple solution, that Paul didn't meet Clement until after coming himself to Rome, doesn't seem likely. The apostle knew all the other church leaders by reputation at least, and Clement himself mentions a deep and long-term friendship with St. Paul in the *Epistle of Clement*. Therefore the question remains: why not send particular greetings to Clement and his church, especially when it was likely the largest one in 1st-century Rome?

Answers to these intriguing questions may possibly be found in the history and archaeology of San Clemente.

Why so much reference to slavery in *Romans*?

Even if he was young at the time *Romans* was penned, Clement was very likely the primary leader of Clemens' large *domus ecclesia* in Rome. No other explanation is as viable. Archaeology from beneath the basilica, testimony of our few extant sources, and immediate veneration of the site combine to declare that St. Clement pastored a church there. As discussed earlier, whether the site we now see was Clemens's home or a government building has no bearing on St. Clement's role as a leader in the church that gathered there.

If, as New Testament scholar J. B. Lightfoot and others surmise, St. Clement was a Hellenized Jewish slave who converted to Christianity and eventually earned his freedom, then mention of slavery in the epistle makes great sense. In fact, *Romans* would be the perfect place to use slavery as an image. No other 1st-century church of which we are aware was led by a freed slave. Given the church leader's background, slavery was a keen literary and illustrative tool.

Further, as a slave, Clement would not have been subject to the Jewish deportations from Rome under Emperor Claudius (r. 41–54). This fits with an early date (perhaps 56/57) for the crafting of St. Paul's letter to the Romans, as is preferred by many scholars. Without a known church leader remaining in Rome, it becomes difficult to imagine St. Paul sending such an important missive in the 50s. If a slave, Clement would have been allowed to remain in the city when all non-slave Jews were deported.

Some explanation is necessary when discussing Roman slavery, because it was different from what many people think of today when using the word. The Greek word *doulos* is the term used repeatedly in *Romans* and throughout the New Testament. It's what is translated "slave" or "servant." In essence, a *doulos* is a slave who bonds himself or herself to a master.

In the past, Bible translators and teachers often avoided the term "slave" and minimized it. That's why *doulos* is rendered in some English versions as "servant" when the more accurate rendering is "slave." This occurred because well-intentioned Christians were haunted by the images of evil modern slavery and wanted to distance the Bible from such wickedness. But Roman-era slavery was very different from the modern racial kind. And in avoiding the seriousness of *doulos*, we have left out something significant.

In an attempt to recapture some of the meaning, Doug Greenwold explains part of the Roman slavery background behind *doulos*:

> When Rome conquered your part of the world, you became a Roman subject without rights. Thus if you were a bookkeeper, a physician or a teacher in a conquered territory, you knew that becoming a Roman *slave* was the only pathway for you to eventually buy your freedom and become a freedman with Roman citizen rights. Given that, it is not surprising that many professionals in conquered lands willingly sold themselves into Roman slavery as the only pathway to Roman citizenship and freedom.[26]

To be sure, the conditions and treatment of slaves varied and for many, if not most slaves, brutality was the norm. *Doulos* is slavery, not merely servanthood. Yet, for some, it was also a pathway to the most important thing one could possess in the 1st-century

Mediterranean world—Roman citizenship. That helps explain why St. Paul uses this word picture. To St. Paul, the most important thing in any and every era is to be a citizen of heaven. For example, consider his majestic statement in *Romans* 6: "But now, since you have been set free from sin and have become enslaved to God, you have your fruit, which results in sanctification—and the outcome is eternal life! For the wages of sin is death, but the gift of God is eternal life in Christ Jesus our Lord."[27] Thus, Christians are willingly Jesus's slaves who move into the eternal freedom that He fought for and won through His death and resurrection. If you have trusted Jesus as Savior, this is who you are. You are God's slave. And He is the ultimate and best Master, granting eternal life in heavenly citizenship.

In contrast, scripture describes the pre-Christian as *doulos* to sin, Satan, or a world system antagonistic to God. St. Paul uses such images earlier in *Romans* 6, detailing the change from *doulos* to sin to *doulos* of God's righteousness, saying: "But thank God that, although you used to be slaves of sin, you obeyed from the heart that pattern of teaching you were transferred to, and having been liberated from sin, you became enslaved to righteousness."[28]

It is hard for us to grasp today, but a *doulos* could have standing in Roman culture. A male slave could buy and sell and run business affairs in his master's name. He was trusted as the master's representative in the marketplace precisely because the *doulos* had chosen to be permanently bonded to that master. A person like that cared only what the master said and was sure to follow the master's instructions.

Given St. Clement's facility with Hebrew and Greek, he was obviously learned. If a slave, he fits the profile of one who would have chosen to become a *doulos*.

Why so much reference to Judaism in *Romans*?

The catacombs give physical confirmation of what historical sources tell us—that as the center of the empire, the city of Rome housed a wide variety of Jews and Gentiles. When these disparate people came to faith in Messiah Jesus, they found themselves unified in ways never previously imagined. As Paul writes to the church in Ephesus: "For He [Jesus] is our peace, who made both groups one and tore down the dividing wall of hostility."[29]

Yet these Jews and Gentiles still had to live with each other in harmony, a task that generations of people have found easier to expound in theory than to live in practice. Given that difficulty, it's not surprising that most of the gatherings listed in *Romans* 16 appear to be homogenous, at least in leadership. Paul lists Greek names, Roman names, and Jewish names as leaders of the various churches. Yet the *domus ecclesia* in our study boasted as broad a leadership team as is imaginable—a Roman citizen of the imperial family and a (possibly) freed Jewish slave. It's reasonable to assume that the church they led had a wide variety of membership.

Thus, to St. Clement and his church, *Romans* chapters 9–11 are no odd interpolation in the text. This is the core of their experience. Certainly, that would have been true to some degree for all churches in the 1st century and beyond. The imagery in the text of rooting Gentiles onto the olive tree of Judaism and Abraham's covenant was especially significant in cosmopolitan Rome. And nowhere would this issue have had more bearing than the church led by Clement and likely including Titus Flavius Clemens. Far from the "strange insertion" as some Bible commentators label it, *Romans* 9–11 is important for their understanding of race relations and God's sovereign plan.

Why no mention of St. Clement in *Romans*?

This is the question that plagued me for some time. At least five groups of Christians, perhaps comprising seven clusters, are mentioned with names in the closing section of St Paul's letter in *Romans* 16, yet there is no mention of Clement.[30] Basilica di San Clemente has much to tell us regarding the book of *Romans*. So, why doesn't the book of *Romans* have anything to say regarding Basilica di San Clemente? I was pondering this during one long afternoon as I studied deep in the lowest level of the building. Having just finished another tour through the site, I sat on the cold floor of the 1st-century structure, alone with my Bible, a notebook, and the continual splashing burble of the underground spring.

This was before tourism had much impact there, and the spaces around me were quiet. The minimal lighting (since expanded) shone softly and warm on the ancient walls. The scents of fresh water and old tufa marble filled the air. In the softness of the setting, I felt somehow more connected to those who had worshipped there long before.

The closed nature of the site gave a sense of what our forebears experienced, since many of their meetings were conducted with caution and some with secrecy. The floor on which I sat and thought had a naturally fine layer of sand, which approximated the street-level situation of pedestrians entering the facility in the 1st century. It was a remarkable moment for me. Though resting some 30 feet under modern ground and able to look around thanks to modern electric lights, it was easy to imagine an oil-lamplit gathering of Christians listening to the reading of the Apostle Paul's letter sent to the Roman churches. In that moment, I opened the scriptures and reread *Romans*.

In the middle of chapter 16, a thought suddenly sprang to my mind. Perhaps Clement's church wasn't mentioned *because they were the original recipients of the letter!* In chapter 16, St. Paul sends greetings to various Christian gatherings in the massive city of Rome. One doesn't say, "Greet Rufus, Aquila, and yourself." No, an author writing an epistle intended to be passed around gives direct instructions to the distributor. He or she only lists the people to whom it should go, since there is no need to mention the one holding the first copy. Obviously, they don't need mentioning because they are the original addressees for the scroll.

I stood with excitement and scanned again the greetings in chapter 16. I wrote in my notes, "Paul sends greetings to each of the house churches in Rome—Priscilla and Aquilla's, Aristobulus', Narcissus', etc.—except the one that was led by Clement! Why leave that one out unless it was clearly the original address? In other words, perhaps the epistle does not mention Clement simply because he and his church were the original recipients! The others are mentioned expressly so Clement will pass the scripture on to them."

Reeling with this thought, I leaned against the wall. I peered around the simple open space as if seeing it for the first time. There was a reasonable chance that I was standing where the letter to the *Romans* was first read aloud. What New Testament scholar F. F. Bruce rightly calls the *summa theologiae* of the Bible may have first been heard right in this room. That possibility overwhelmed me. I slumped back to the floor and began rereading *Romans* from the start. About chapter 4, I stood and began reading aloud, picturing our forefathers listening to new scripture given by God through His apostle. It was one of the most thrilling experiences of my life.

Please do not misunderstand. God is omnipresent. Unlike some religions, Christians are not superstitiously tied to sacred spaces. Christianity is based on the sacrificial death and resurrection of Jesus Christ the eternal Son of God, not the limitations of time and space. Yet time and space are significant because they help us understand the context of scripture. Christians acknowledge that the history of Christianity is rooted physically in geography and the lives of peoples throughout the centuries. Thus, places like San Clemente affect our understanding of biblical context and are physical reminders that God works daily in the lives of people and has done so throughout history.

The person and work of St. Clement in light of Basilica di San Clemente

With this possibility in mind regarding the recipient of St. Paul's letter, it is helpful to review what we know of St. Clement. Having discussed all these points in the previous chapter, bullet reminders will suffice here:

- Of the many early churches in Rome, only St. Clement's church maintained an unbroken legacy over the first five centuries of Christianity. Other *domus ecclesiae* were appreciated and remembered. However, San Clemente was recognized in a different manner. It was venerated as the place where Christianity flourished during the dark times that arose in the mid- and late-1st-century AD.

- In *Philippians* 4:3, St. Paul calls St. Clement his fellow worker. This was written as the Apostle Paul endured his first imprisonment in Rome, ca. AD 61.

- St. Clement was later considered the leader and bishop of the churches in Rome, though it is doubtful that the title held the same meaning in the 1st century as we give it today. He does appear to be the primary figure in the churches of Rome and was the author of the *First Epistle of Clement* (*1 Clement*) written to a church in Corinth, likely at the end of the 1st century.

- In his letter, St. Clement feels very comfortable speaking as an authoritative leader; for example in his exposition of *Romans* chapter 13.

1 *Clement* in light of Basilica di San Clemente

St. Clement's epistle to Christians in Corinth certainly affects our understanding of the basilica. Likewise, our interpretation of the letter is shaped by the context of St. Clement's leadership. Sadly, nothing at the site of his ministry sheds light on the date of *1 Clement*. That remains an open question with a vocal minority favoring dates as early as the 60s, and a majority arguing that AD 93–96 fits best.[31] Below are observations from the letter most useful to our understanding of St. Clement and his church.

- The famous 19th-century German theologian and historian Adolph von Harnack described *1 Clement* as "the most important document we have received from earliest Christianity."[32]

- The style and language of *1 Clement* is an intricate combination of natural Hebraisms and Hellenic thought.

Harnack is on point in stating, "The Letter is, from a language point of view, influenced by two literary tones, as it were, one of which is the Hebraic 'tone' (LXX) and one of which is the Greek 'tone' (rhythmic prose)."[33] The epistle contains many Old Testament references to unity and order. Yet it boasts very Hellenized illustrations of the resurrection, including all nature and the phoenix.[34]

- The main issue addressed in the letter is submission to local church leaders. Interestingly, St. Clement uses the Greek word *presbyteros* to describe these elders, not *episkopos*. Each is used in the New Testament of church leaders. *Episkopos* is often translated "bishop" and means "overseer." This is someone providing high-level overwatch, dealing with policy and direction. By contrast, *presbyteros* is a term used for the typical leaders of a village, a familiar idea to Mediterranean people and especially important to understanding the Old Testament. In his *episkopos* role, an elder cannot become engrossed in ministry details lest he lose the perspective needed for oversight. (See *Acts* 6 for an early example.) In the *presbyteros* function, an elder is actively engaged in community life. The use of *presbyteros* in plural indicates that Clement is addressing local elders and not hierarchical bishops, which may not have existed yet.

- St. Clement also references an "established and internal succession" of leaders in the Corinthian church. Lightfoot seems correct in seeing this as evidence of localized authority in each church. Interestingly, Harnack, who disagreed with Lightfoot on much of *1 Clement*'s meaning, concurred.

- An early date for *1 Clement* fits well with what we know of the author's activity in the fifties and sixties of the 1st century. It also allows for him to be an older man when he first accepts the "shepherd" role at Clemens's *domus ecclesia*. However, the references to "calamities" in *1 Clement* fit better the Domitian persecution of the 90s.

- *1 Clement* specifically mentions the book we reference as *1 Corinthians*, referring to it as St. Paul's first letter to that church. This adds an intriguing angle to the discussion of whether that epistle was indeed the first one the apostle sent to Corinth. Clement also alludes to other New Testament books, referencing *Hebrews* most often, followed by *Romans* and *Titus*.

- The epistle contains a "call to worship" prayer similar to *Revelation* 4:8. This is possibly an indication of widespread worship practice and is certainly understandable coming from the pen of an influential pastor.

- *1 Clement* claims that St. Paul did indeed go far west, reaching Spain and possibly Britain. *Romans* chapter 15 declares that to be Paul's intention, including a promise to visit the recipient church on his way. Though we have no corroboration for such a journey between St. Paul's imprisonments, one is hard pressed to devise a reason for St. Clement to fabricate such a tale.

- The epistle from St. Clement was long respected in Corinth. We know that it was still being read publicly in Corinth in AD 170 and may have continued being read in the Corinthian churches for generations after its AD 170 attestation.

- Scholars' conclusions regarding *1 Clement* are interestingly diverse. St. Ignatius of Loyola (1491–1556) claimed the letter was clearly penned by a pope who held sway over all other bishops. J. B. Lightfoot declared the text was crafted by a Hebrew, likely a former slave. While not disputing *1 Clement*'s Hebraisms, church historian Henry Chadwick stated that the letter was so Hellenic that Clement served as one of the first to link Athens and Jerusalem. There is probably some truth to each of these.

- Chapters 12–16 of *Romans* have remarkable contrasts between the imperative mood verb of a command and the indicative mood verb of an assertion, opinion, or question. Since *1 Clement* occasionally employs this same technique, it is useful to view Clement's Pauline inspiration, which speaks strongly to their relationship.[35]

Romans	*Imperative command*	*Indicative statement*
12:1–2	"Present your bodies"	"The mercies of God"
12:3–11	"Serve the Lord"	"God has given to each"
13:1–7	"Give what is due"	"Authorities are established by God"
14:1–9	"Wake up"	"Time is short"
16:1–16	"Greet"	"The churches greet you"
16:17–27	"Turn from dividers"	"God will crush Satan"

- Even farther afield, the early-20th-century Latin scholar Elmer Merrill asserted that such a person as St. Clement probably never existed. While Merrill is singular and almost surely inaccurate in his assertion that St. Clement is fictitious, his comments are not all worthless. In his *Essays in Early Christian History,* he reminds us that, "It should always be remembered that a 'unanimous ancient tradition,' of which we often hear so much in modern historical discussion, may often mean nothing more than that an attractive but baseless conjecture made by some one writer gained general credence among non-critical successors who had no other source of knowledge on the subject."[36]

The *Epistle to the Romans* in light of Basilica di San Clemente

The occasion of the *Letter to the Romans*:

By late A.D. 56, St. Paul had been ministering with great success in Ephesus for years. The great Jerusalem church offering and the establishment of churches in the East had each been completed. St. Paul then finds his heart drawn west. He desires to go to Rome & then on to Spain. It is obvious that St. Paul has had much contact with the churches in Rome through various friends including Aquilla and Priscilla, whom he met when they were expelled from Rome with the other free Jews. The apostle may be desiring that Rome become a sort of Antioch of the West—a base of financial support and a start for mission trips. In order to prepare the people for that purpose, Paul puts down for them on paper his *summa evangelion*—his summary of the good news he has preached as God's apostle. This is the message he trusted some church—likely the one headed by St. Clement—to disseminate.

The recipients of the *Letter to the Romans*:

We may be fair in saying that when St. Paul wrote *Romans*, the Christian community in Rome that comprised both Jewish and Gentile Christians and at least one church (likely the largest one) was led by St. Clement. Like other churches, each Roman congregation was called an *ekklesia*—the Greek term for (among other things) the popular assembly in municipal governments. Christianity in other cities began among Jews and there is no reason to assume Rome was any different. Following the pattern of the Pauline missions, we can surmise that "God fearers," Gentiles who were interested in Judaism and attended synagogue without becoming Jews, were the first non-Jew denizens of Rome to be attracted to Christianity. We know from Roman records that these early converts were from a wide swath of social classes, with a sprinkling of the lower classes and regular additions from the rich. Slaves were welcomed among the assembly; no attempt was made to liberate them, but they were comforted by the promise of a future kingdom in which all could be free.

The author of the *Letter to the Romans*:

There exists a great deal of misunderstanding about the person and ministry of the Apostle Paul. The plethora of inaccurate teaching seems traceable to two great errors, each of which is countered by what we have learned from St. Clement:

- Some ignore St. Paul's Jewish roots. Those trapped in this mindset sadly miss the Hebraic foundation upon which *Romans* is built. As shown above, this limits the understanding considerably. Particularly, the arguments in *Romans* demand some foreknowledge of both the Abrahamic and Mosaic covenants. Some 19th-century and 20th-century teachers tended to approach the text from an exclusively Roman-modern perspective and thus missed critical Hebraic ideas. Particularly pertinent concepts include what Jewish Paul means by the Spirit vs. flesh and what adoption into God's family entails (see, *Letter to the Romans* 8:15, 9:26, and *Letter to the Galatians* 3:26).

- Some reduce St. Paul to a Hebrew-only teacher focused on community and not on individual justification by faith. These teachers make the apostle a caricature. *Romans* must be understood as intended, penned by a master in Greek thought and Roman law—something some popular modern teachers strive to ignore. New Testament scholar F. F. Bruce's comments on "Judaizers" in *Galatians* and *Romans* seem eerily fitting for those who claim Paul teaches salvation by "association" in a Hebraic style covenant community: "This teaching nullfie[s] the principle that salvation is bestowed by grace and received by faith; it gives men a share in that saving glory which, according to Paul's gospel, belongs to God alone."[37]

The contents of the *Letter to the Romans*:

Based on St. Clement, his church, and his writings, *Romans* should be studied with these concepts in mind:

- Understanding Roman slavery is critical to proper interpretation of chapters 1–6.

- As previously mentioned, the racial background of Roman churches in general and the *domus ecclesia* under Basilica di San Clemente in particular aid greatly in seeing chapters 9–11 in context.

- Knowing something of the functions of the house churches, one is better prepared to appreciate chapters 12–16. Learning about St. Clement and the first churches is helpful whether each individual greeted in *Romans* is a church host and/or shepherd (as some think), or if the number of churches is limited to San Clemente plus those specifically addressed with the formula "the church in their house."

The impact of the *Letter to the Romans*:

The importance of understanding the issues in *Romans* is hard to overstate. Protestant reformer Martin Luther (1483–1546) is certainly not a favored son of Rome, but he is laudable for his appreciation of St. Paul's *Letter to the Romans*. Whatever one thinks of Luther, the first words of his introduction to the Roman epistle are memorable: "[*Romans*] is worthy not only that every Christian should know it word for word, by heart, but occupy himself with it every day, as the daily bread of the soul. It can never be read or pondered too much, and the more it is dealt with the more precious it becomes, and the better it tastes."[38]

Though *1 Clement* is not canonical (part of the books commonly accepted as those comprising the Bible; rather it is part of the collection known as the *Apostolic Fathers*), the book is significant as a shaper of souls and a very important writing of the early church. That's why Adolf von Harnack's note to his professorial colleagues regarding *I Clement* contains this summary: "From the first to the last page, this fundamental character...of highest solemnity and great vitality...is powerfully expressed in the letter [of *I Clement*] and one must look to the resolute morality of the puritans of England and of New England before you will find again in common religion a place where the sovereignty of God's Holy Laws are accepted so self-evidently."[39]

CONCLUSION

A few years ago, my family happened to be in Rome on a day of special civic history celebrations. Dozens of actors and volunteers entered the Via Sacra, walking from the Colosseum toward the Capitoline Hill. People dressed as centurions and soldiers mingled with vestal virgins and senators. A Pontifex Maximus even appeared, directing the procession toward the Temple of Vesta.

Braudrick children before the Temple of Vesta
Photo by Janna Braudrick

While we all observed, they recreated an ancient ceremony there. Fire from the temple hearth was taken up in four censers. Four groups of officials, each led by a vestal virgin, carried the hearth fire through the traditional four quadrants of the city. In classical times, this was an annual ritual to relight the fires of any homes where the flame had expired. It was considered ancient even during the era of the Roman Republic and celebrated the centrality of the hearth in every home. It also tied the people to the state cult, as one's fire could only be replenished by the servants of the hearth-goddess overseen by the Pontifex Maximus, a state official. Thus, the Roman state provided a basic essential of life for anyone in need.

Over a pizza, our family had a rich discussion of what we had just seen. As often happens in Italy, the occupant of a nearby table overheard our chat and joined in. This delightful fellow was a Roman Catholic priest on short-term assignment in Rome. As we talked, I shared some of my conclusions regarding Basilica di San Clemente. He grew animated, and we became so engrossed in conversation that neither of us noticed as the younger Braudrick children fell asleep on their mother's lap. At the end of our long talk, he shared a pithy summary that may prove helpful to all who walk through the layers of San Clement's churches: "Whether or not you have found the exact place *Romans* was first read, the site is very important. You are right to call all Christians to read both *Romans* in scripture and *1 Clement*, as they speak to the issues raised under San Clemente. And I think it's very possible that San Clemente should inform our understanding of each letter."

The priest was absolutely correct. Likely, we will never have certainty that the 1st-century congregation of the present-day site of Basilica di San Clemente was the receiving congregation of St. Paul's *Epistle to the Romans*. However, there is no reason to doubt the possibility. What we do know for certain is that St.

Paul's New Testament letter and St. Clement's 1st-century letter are foundational documents of Christianity. Sharing common themes and authors who were instrumental in the early church, readers through the centuries have strengthened their own spiritual journeys and pilgrimages by reading and following the words of these writings.

Explore the mysteries and magnificence of Basilica di San Clemente and know that as you do so, you are following in the footsteps of Christians throughout the centuries who have stood where you stand, prayed where you pray, and listened to the words of St. Paul and St. Clement spoken and read in one of Christianity's earliest houses of worship.

APPENDIX A

Mithraism and the Mithraeum

This small book is designed to help the traveler, historian, or student of scripture better understand the churches beneath Basilica di San Clemente. Our goal is to learn what St. Clement and the successive buildings bearing his name contribute to our understanding of the Bible, East-West Christian relations, the letter of St. Clement known as *1 Clement,* and the challenges facing churches throughout the centuries.

However, when we decided upon the title *The Mysteries of San Clemente,* the publisher and I decided that this appendix was necessary to delineate between the mysteries of San Clemente and the mystery religion of Mithraism. Early readers were tantalized by the mithraeum found next to the 4th-century basilica. Since it is accessible via the church site, many visitors to Rome will likewise desire more information on the mithraeum. While not exhaustive, the material below may provide direction for further individual investigation.

Mithraism

Between the seventh and sixth centuries BC, Arian (or Aryan) naturalism in Persia began to transform. A divine hierarchy developed, headed by Ahura Mazda. Though not creator per se, it was believed that Ahura Mazda oversaw all good creation and granted understanding—thus his name, which means "wise lord." He ruled with six manifestations of his power known as the Amesha Spenta. Beneath them were angelic beings who dispensed justice and purity. Their chief was known as Mithras. Over time Mithras became viewed as more godlike and less angelic. He eventually became considered part of the Persian pantheon of deities.

In her book on subterranean Rome, Ivana Della Portella describes the transmogrification of Mithras into Mithraism:

> Originating in Persia, the cult took its name from the Indian and Persian god, Mithras. Always identified in the East with the sun, he was the guarantor of pacts between tribes, the god of oaths, of contracts and all of those forms and conventions of daily life that ensure peace and stability in agricultural settlements. These attributes gradually began to transform him, even in ancient Persia, into a more warlike and military figure, and it is in this new guise that Mithras was to prevail as the religion spread throughout the Roman Empire.[40]

The migration actually began in Greece. When Pompey routed the Cilician pirates in 67 BC, some who worshipped Mithras settled in Attica.[41] There, mystery religions were already well-established, and Mithraism was welcomed. The acceptance came with unspoken and possibly unintended consequences.

While the Mazdaen Mithras served as a redemptive figure, as a mystery religion Mithraism changed. Over the next two centuries, Babylonian liturgies, astrology, borrowings from Christianity, and mysterious legalisms became part of the new religion. His myth finally coalesced into the following story, best told by Portella:

> One day, Mithras, a young and beautiful god, appeared as light out of the solid vault of the sky: *invictus de petra natus*.[42] The rock that had given him life put him down on the banks of a river, under the shade of a sacred tree. Some shepherds witnessed this miraculous birth. They saw him rise out of the rock naked, armed with a knife, a torch in his hand and a Phyrigian cap on his head. They gave him shelter, offering gifts and worshipping him. From the moment of his birth, Mithras began his heroic deeds that sought to subjugate the evil of the cosmos.
>
> He began by challenging the Sun who, defeated, struck up a pact of alliance with him and passed to him his radiant crown, henceforth to be one of Mithras' attributes. Next came the story of the wild bull. Mithras captured the bull and led it into his cave (*specus*), a task that was made more difficult by the numerous obstacles set in his path (*transitus*). The bull managed to escape, however, and was seen by the Sun who sent an order to Mithras by his messenger, the Raven, to kill it.

> Reluctantly, Mithras undertook the task. He set off after the bull, helped by his faithful dog. As the bull was about to take shelter in the cave from which it had escaped, the god seized it by the nostrils and plunged his knife into its side (*tauroctonia*).
>
> Then from the side of the dying bull there miraculously sprang all the beneficial plants that were to inhabit the earth: from its spine came wheat and from its blood the vine. Ahriman, god of Evil, unable to stand passively by in the face of this profusion of life, sent his evil attendants, the scorpion and the snake, to fight the spread of these life-giving forces. But his attempts were in vain, and neither managed to prevent the bull's seed from being shed on the earth, which, aided by the Moon, gave rise to every species of useful animal. Mithras and the Sun sealed their victory with a feast (*agape*), and then, climbing into the Sun's chariot, ascended to the heavens from where Mithras continued to look after the faithful.[43]

Like all mystery religions, Mithraism was shrouded in secrecy. Apparently, some of the *syndexioi* converted to belief in Jesus and provided the early Christian leader Tertullian (ca. 155–ca. 220) with information about the cult. It is from Tertullian's writings against the religion that we have most of our early information about the workings of Mithraism.

Rostrum in the Mithraic triclinium (feast hall) under San Clemente

A person desiring to join the *syndexioi* began working his way up through the levels of knowledge. Each level was tied to one of the seven trials of Mithras and was represented by a spirit. Level one was the Raven; two the Nymph;[44] three the Soldier. Writing around AD 400, the great Bible translator Jerome noted that these first three levels were considered mere servants. The next three: Lion, Persian, and Sun-runner (*heliodromus*) were viewed as participants in the mysteries. In the "schoolroom" of the apartment building next to the 4th-century San Clemente building, niches held images of each of these overseeing spirits. Further, the members of each level would wear masks during ceremonies. These masks were representations of their "spirit" and the wearer would make noises appropriate to their masks. (Raven seems fairly straightforward, but one cannot help but wonder what a chrysalis/nymph or a *heliodromus* sounded like.)

The seventh and final level was the Father (*Pater*). At each stage, the participant was expected to shed a particular emotion. This purportedly allowed the soul to reach a kind of "apathy" similar to the Stoics. Each level demanded investment of time

The Mithraic school

and money to enter. Each necessitated hard work to learn the secret "knowledge" (*gnosis*) necessary to level-up. At the seventh level one became "spiritual" and the father of one's own fate. Advancement was predicated on conquering emotions.

Mithraism operated in secret and this was achieved in part via caves. Each Mithraeum was established in a cave or a structure made to resemble a cave. This design provided secrecy and mimicked the cavern of Mithras's baptism in the blood of the bull—the *taurobolium*. The main room was carved into a *triclinium,* the typical three-side feast arrangement of all Roman lands, and a *rostrum* (podium) with an image of Mithras was placed in the center.

The triclinium hosted the most important communal practice of the *syndexioi,* a great feast. First, the members would partake of the intoxicating extract of the divine haoma plant as incense filled the chamber. Then, platters of foods would be enjoyed along with heavy wines. Probably borrowing from the early Christians' descriptions of their Lord's Last Supper, Mithraism eventually dubbed this "the loving fellowship (*agape*) feast."

Early Christian Responses

Early Christian apologist Justin Martyr (ca. 100–ca. 165) responded to this Mithraic co-opting of Christian terminology, writing, "In imitation [of communion] the evil daemons have laid it down that the same shall be done in the mysteries of Mithras: for the bread and a cup of water are presented with certain words."[45] Tertullian's response to the cult is also instructive. He notes that "Mithras liturgy is celebrated in hidden caves where deep in the darkness and obscurity they can escape the benediction of the bright sun." He then launches into a contrast of Mithraism and its "kingdom of shades" (*castra tenebrarum*) with Christianity's "kingdom of light" (*castra lucis*).[46]

Scripture provides a strong response as well. Part of the Apostle Paul's motive in using the word "mystery" is to expose the distinctions between Christianity and mystery religions. For example, in St. Paul's New Testament letter to the *Colossians,* he refers to: "...the mystery hidden for ages and generations but now revealed to his saints. To them God chose to make known how great among the Gentiles are the riches of the glory of this mystery, which is Christ in you, the hope of glory."[47]

The key word is *mysterion,* a Greek term we translate "mystery." To understand mysterion, consider the murder mystery genre that has become very popular over the past 200 years. My all-time favorites are the Nero Wolfe mysteries written by Rex Stout. I own all 75 of them and have read each at least three times. The dialogue is sparkling; the vocabulary brilliant; the characters so real that I am not convinced that Nero and Archie and Fritz and Saul don't live today in some lost corner of New York City.

But the best part of the Nero Wolfe mysteries is that they are *solvable.* When Nero Wolfe, the master genius, reveals the truth at the dénouement you always sit back and say, "Oh my goodness! It was there all along. Why didn't I see that?" Now, the plot is so intricate that no one except my wife and Nero Wolfe ever figures out who committed the murder, but the possibility is there. This is a far cry from murder mysteries where one is surprised by some twist that had nothing to do with the story and just pops up at the end.

Mysterion is like a Nero Wolfe mystery. It doesn't mean a surprise. It indicates something that was there on stage all along but not fully understood until the master revealed its significance.

Jesus is the Jewish Messiah; yet He has always had Gentiles in His plan. As Master of all, He reveals that truth in this new economy of the church age. Christians—whether Jewish or Gentile in origin—know this. It has been made clear to them. They understand what Jesus was saying when He told a Jewish audience, "I have other sheep, which are not of this fold; I must bring them also, and they will hear My voice; and they will become one flock *with* one shepherd."[48]

Some, reading St. Paul's writings, mistakenly claim that in his New Testament *Letter to the Colossians,* St. Paul is equating Christianity with mystery religions like Mithraism. Nothing could be more untrue. In a mystery religion there is no grace. There is no justification by faith. In fact, mystery religion followers had to work and earn their way through various levels in order to have a chance for salvation. St. Paul is not equating Mithraism and Christianity; he is attacking the foundational ideas of religions like Mithraism.

The central idea in St. Paul's letter *Colossians* has nothing in common with Demeter or Mithras or other mystery religions. Paul's *mysterion* is more simple and free and ancient—the Gentiles can be rescued by faith in the Jewish Messiah. That's why many thinkers through the centuries have called the related paragraph in *Colossians* the height of all Christian thought. It captures what makes believers in Jesus different now and forever:

> If then you have been raised with Christ, seek the things that are above, where Christ is, seated at the right hand of God. Set your minds on things that are above, not on things that are on earth. For you have died, and your life is hidden with Christ in God. When Christ who is your life appears, then you also will appear with him in glory.[49]

"Hidden" in verse 3 represents one of the most clever wordplays in the Bible. In one sense it's straightforward encouragement—you are hidden in Christ, so there's no need to worry about this life or even death. One can certainly fix the mind on that encouragement, yet there's more. In another sense, St. Paul is attacking the mystery religion cults that plagued Colossae and the entire Roman world. Mystical legalists, these initiates to secret societies liked to boast about how they had a "fuller" spiritual life because of the mysterious things hidden in their secret traditions. The word they used most often for their secret knowledge was a form *krypto*—the term we translate "hidden."

St. Paul takes their special word and uses it against them. William Barclay's summary is brilliant: "It is as if Paul said, 'For you the treasures of wisdom are hidden in your secret books; for us Christ is the treasury of wisdom and we are hidden in him.'"[50] St. Paul declares in essence, "You can have your old dead traditions. We have a living God."

Appropriately, St. Paul's letter to Christians in Rome also addresses this, especially the pagan idea that religion was ritualistic repetition. He writes:

> So then as through one transgression there resulted condemnation to all men, even so through one act of righteousness there resulted justification of life to all men. For as through the one man's disobedience the many were made sinners, even so through the obedience of the One the many will be made righteous.

> The Law came in so that the transgression would increase; but where sin increased, grace abounded all the more, so that, as sin reigned in death, even so grace would reign through righteousness to eternal life through Jesus Christ our Lord. [51]

Ritual and law were very important in pagan cults, as Lesley and Roy Adkins point out:

> The smallest mistake in performance would render a ritual invalid. Many rituals had been handed down unchanged, and gradually their meaning became forgotten, so that in later times they were barely understood. Rituals were occasionally performed to honor gods whose character and attributes had been forgotten, with only the name of the god surviving.[52]

St. Paul spent the beginning of the Roman letter describing the Lord's attributes, and this seems to reveal why. Roman people had a cultural predisposition to forget the nature of God, only recollecting ritual. Of course, every era struggles with such empty traditionalism. It can be seen vividly in Roman churches today and is by no means absent from the church where I worship in the United States. Yet, the mystery religions upped the ante in their exaltation of rote repetition.

Remember, mystery religions demanded that the one desiring salvation learn a difficult set of information and study for years to become initiated. Once initiated, the person was not permanently saved. He had to keep going regularly through the rituals in order to stay saved. The key was repetition. If one missed the repetition, one lost salvation.

For example, consider the one repetitious ceremony of Mithraism about which we have some knowledge—the re-sacrifice of the bull. Once a man—and it was men since women were largely, if not totally, excluded from Mithraism—learned enough to become initiated, he had to regularly be re-bathed in the blood of a bull in order to stay "saved."[53]

The initiation baptism of *taurobolium* brought a soul up to a salvific "0." However, if one didn't keep up the repetition of practices demanded by Mithraism, one dropped back below the salvation line. Thus, the relative context of *Romans* is that it was written to people living in a culture that viewed ritual and repetition as the ways to connect with God. Given the fact that millions of people mistakenly live today as if such were the case, Paul's words apply as much to our world as to Rome. Mithraism may be gone, but the human desire to earn our own salvation apart from grace continues.

Continual Challenge

Remember, the Mithraeum was across an alley from the Clement church and was in no way connected to either the 1st or 4–5th-century basilicas. However, it is chilling to realize how the practices of the dead mystery religion parallel unbiblical nonsense that can creep into the churches of Jesus. One imagines a toxic gas seeping out of a back alley and into a healthy home. So can traditionalism leach in and overwhelm the tradition of Christianity, turning it into mere traditionalism. Regarding such, the reminder from Yale professor Jaroslav Pelikan is useful: "Tradition is the living faith of the dead. Traditionalism is the dead faith of the living."[54]

The Apostle Paul warns against the dead traditionalism in paganism, Mithraism, coming Gnosticism, etc. The final words of his first letter to Timothy warn: "Timothy, guard what has been entrusted to you, avoiding irreverent, empty speech and contradictions from the 'knowledge' that falsely bears that name. By professing it, some people have deviated from the faith. Grace be with all of you."[55]

This reminder is so important that it is mentioned last, where it will be most likely remembered. John is also concerned that Christians not be turned to worship anything but the Triune God. Thus, he ends his first epistle by commanding, "Little children, guard yourselves from idols."[56] Again, the placement is significant. Of course, idols are not always ancient. They have plagued each generation since Eden.

The mysteries of San Clemente throw down a powerful challenge—not only to explore the past, but to learn from it. This is a continual challenge, and I pray the mysteries and lessons of San Clemente help you as they have helped me.

APPENDIX B

Glossary

Apse – It is a large semicircular or polygonal recess in a church or basilica, arched or with a domed or semi-domed roof, typically at the eastern end, and usually containing the altar.

Basilica – It was initially a Roman public building, usually with double colonnades, serving multiple official functions including courts of law. After Constantine's rule, most churches were constructed on the basilica plan. Not all churches are basilicas. In Roman Catholicism and Greek Orthodoxy, it is a canonical title of honor given to church buildings that are important due to their antiquity or by their role as international houses of worship based on their association with a major saint, an important historical event, or, in the Orthodox Church, a national patriarch.

Catacombs – Subterranean passageways were used as a place of burial in ancient Rome. An area called "the Hollows" was riddled with passages where the tufa rock had eroded into passages. Churches began meeting there and in similar places around the city. By the late 2nd century, deep communal underground tombs were being carved out in response to a Senate ban on traditional burials inside the city limits due to fears of plague. There are at least thirty-nine Christian catacombs in Rome.

Cloaca Maxima – It was an ancient Roman sewer constructed in the 6th century BC. Its primary function was to carry away storm water from the Forum district to the Tiber River.

domus ecclesiae – It is a term for the earliest places of Christian gatherings for worship, sponsored or hosted by wealthy Christians in homes and larger villas.

Great Schism of 1054 – Also known as the East-West Schism, this was the splitting of Christianity in the 11th century between Western (Roman Catholic) and Eastern (Eastern Orthodox) Christianity. It occurred due to doctrinal and sociopolitical differences as well as the rejection of universal papal authority by Eastern Church patriarchs.

Mithraeum (sometimes spelled mithreum) – It is a temple-type space dedicated to the mystery religion Mithraism. Most are located in the Roman Empire, as the religion became a distinctly Roman form of Persian Zoroastrianism, and most were constructed between AD 100 and 300. Some were housed in caverns altered for worship while others were placed in buildings in imitation of a cave, as is the case in the apartment building at the lowest level of San Clemente.

Mithraism – It is a Roman mystery religion based on the god Mithras. Loosely based on the Zoroastrian god Mithra, the Roman version was decidedly different from its predecessor. As a mystery religion, "salvation" was earned through levels of learning, and revealing the mysteries to outsiders was forbidden. The religion appears to have been popular in certain Roman Army legions. From literature and archaeology we know very little; only that Mithras was born out of a rock, slaughtered a bull whose blood brought enlightenment, and shared a meal with Sol, the sun god.

Narthex – It refers to the indoor entry hall or outdoor portico leading into the nave of a basilica.

Nave – It is the central aisle of a basilica. In churches, this was the main gathering place of worshippers during the Christian assembly.

Syndexioi – The word literally means "ones united in the handshake," and is a self-reference of adherents of Mithraism.

Tengrism (or Tengerism) – This is an ancient Central Asian religion that is a syncretized mix of shamanism, ancestor worship, animism, and polytheism. It worships Tengri, a supreme power associated with the sky.

Triclinium – It is a three-sided seating area used for large gatherings and ceremonial meals.

Writings

1 Clement – This is an early Christian writing by St. Clement that was written about AD 96 from Rome to Christians in Corinth. Though not part of the Bible, it is an important piece of patristic literature written by an Apostolic Father.

Epistle to the Colossians – This is one of the books of the New Testament and one of St. Paul's letters to early Christians. It was likely written in the autumn of AD 61 to Christians at Colossae, a small city about 100 miles east of Ephesus.

Epistle to the Romans – This is one of the books of the New Testament and one of St. Paul's letters to early Christians. Likely written in the late 50s (probably winter of AD 56/57), the original recipients of St. Paul's letter may have been Christians worshipping at the site that is now Basilica di San Clemente.

People

Adrian II (Pope, b. 792, d. 872) – He approved the use of the Slavic language in liturgy by Saints Cyril and Methodius.

Basil I (811–886) – He was Byzantine emperor 867–886.

St. Clement (d. AD 99) – Known as an Apostolic Father (along with Polycarp and Ignatius of Antioch), he was a pastor in Rome during the latter half of the 1st c. AD Attested by Tertullian as bishop of Rome, he was the author of a letter to the Corinthian church known as *1 Clement*. He is likely the Clement mentioned by the Apostle Paul in his *Epistle to the Philippians* chapter 4.

St. Cyril (826–869) – He was one of two brothers (Cyril and Methodius) sent from Constantinople as Christian missionaries to the Slavs. They devised the Glagolitic alphabet for Slavic languages and rendered the New Testament into the new form. Later, they went to Rome, where Cyril died. The Orthodox Church considers them "equal to the Apostles," and in 1980 the Roman Catholic Church declared them "co-patron saints of Europe" along with St. Benedict.

Cyrus II (b. 590 to 580 BC, d. ca. 529 BC) – Also known as Cyrus the Great, he was the founder of the Achaemenid Empire, the first Persian empire.

De Rossi, Giovanni Battista (Carlo) (1822–1894) – Known by many as the "Father of Christian archaeology," he was an Italian archaeologist who did some of the earliest excavation work at Basilica di San Clemente along with Fr. Joseph Mullooly.

Domitian (Roman emperor, b. AD 51, d. AD 96) – He was one of the most brutal Roman emperors and reigned from AD 81–96. Jews and Christians were heavily persecuted in the years of his reign.

John VII (Patriarch, b. end of 8th c. and d. ca. 843–863) – Also known as Grammaticus ("the Grammarian"), he was the Patriarch of Constantinople.

Justin Martyr (b. ca. 100, d. ca. 165) – He was an early Christian apologist and philosopher of the 2nd-century. Martyred for his faith, he was later canonized.

St. Methodius (815–885) – He was one of two brothers (Cyril and Methodius) sent from Constantinople as Christian missionaries to the Slavs. They devised the Glagolitic alphabet for Slavic languages and rendered the New Testament into the new form. Later, they went to Rome, where Cyril died. The Orthodox Church considers them "equal to the Apostles," and in 1980 the Roman Catholic Church declared them "co-patron saints of Europe" along with St. Benedict.

Michael III (Byzantine emperor, b. 840, d. 862) – He ruled from 842 until his assassination. His parents were Theodora and Theophilus. He is known primarily for his restoration of the use of icons in the Byzantine Church, and successful campaigns against the Arabs and Slavs.

Mullooly, Joseph (1812–1880) – He was an Irish Dominican priest who served at Basilica di San Clemente beginning in 1852. Along with archaeologist Giovanni Battista (Carlo) de Rossi, he was instrumental in excavating and recovering the early history of the basilica.

Nabonidus (r. 556 BC to 539 BC) – He was the last emperor of the Neo-Babylonian Empire.

Nebuchadnezzar (ca. 630 to ca. 562 BC) – Also known as Nebuchadnezzar II, he was the second and greatest king of the Chaldean dynasty of Babylonia, reigning from 605 BC until his death.

Nicholas I (Pope, b. ca. 800, d. 867) – Later, St. Nicholas I, his papal reign was from 858 to 867. He exerted decisive influence upon the historical development of the papacy and its position and authority among the Christian nations of Western Europe.

Photios (Patriarch, b. ca. 820, d. ?) – Also known as Photios I or Photios the Great, and later St. Photios; he was Patriarch of Constantinople from 858–867 and 877–886.

Pius IX (Pope, b. 1792, d. 1878) – His papal reign was from 1846–1878. He was the last pope who functioned as a secular ruler and monarch of the Papal States from 1846–1870.

Ramsay, Sir William M. (1851–1939) – He was a Scottish archaeologist and New Testament scholar known for his writings on early Christianity.

Tertullian (b. ca. 155/160, d. 220) – He was an important early Christian theologian and polemicist.

Theophilos (Emperor, b. ca. 812, d. 842) – He was Byzantine emperor from 829–842.

Titus Flavius Clemens (AD 50–95) – He was a cousin of the Emperor Domitian and the husband of Flavia Domitilla. He briefly served as consul under the rule of his cousin, but Domitian condemned him to death for "godlessness." Early pagan sources claim that Titus Flavius Clemens converted to Judaism, but later Christian sources say he became a follower of Jesus. Given the 1st-century Roman confusion between the two, the latter seems more likely. His wife appears to be the same Domitilla who was martyred as a Christian for refusing to sacrifice to idols.

Titus (Roman emperor, b. AD 9, d. AD 79) – Also known as Vespasian, he was a Roman emperor who reigned from AD 69 to 79. Titus consolidated and brought political stability to the empire.

Theodora (Empress, d. 548) – She was married to Justinian and served as one of his chief advisers.

Theoktistos (d. 855) – He was regent for Michael III and adviser to Empress Theodora.

ENDNOTES

1 Note: Though this study covers a wide range of eras and topics, I have chosen to forgo the usual academic footnoting. This was a difficult decision, knowing that it may limit the use of this book in academia. Nonetheless, it is the best option to ensure that laypeople can appreciate the discovery of San Clemente and that I can actually complete this history before another layer of rubble is added to the site. A bibliography is provided for those wanting to dig further. A professor friend, knowing my anguish over this choice, comforted me by saying, "If Thucydides and Luke could claim to have researched extensively and offer no source notes, you certainly can. I know you, and your veracity falls somewhere between those two."

2 A good summary of the theological and political stress is found in *The Kidnapping of Edgardo Mortara* by David Kertzer.

3 If you wish to study this movement, Nancy Pearcey does an excellent job detailing the changes in her book *Saving Leonardo.*

4 Note that "imperial" after roughly AD 450 always refers to the Roman court at Constantinople. When the western empire succumbed to internal and external pressures, it "fell." Meanwhile, the eastern empire continued for another 1000 years. For clarity, most early modern historians referred to this eastern empire as "Byzantine," yet the citizens of that great state still considered themselves Roman.

5 The Orthodox Patriarch is the Archbishop considered "first among peers." Some compare the idea to Octavian's self-designation of Principate—first citizen—of the Roman Republic.

6 Methodios I, whom we last encountered in that supreme role, was succeeded by one Ignatios. The Queen Mother Theodora personally selected Ignatios for the position. Ten years later, Michael III abolished

the regency and removed not only his mother but Ignatios. Michael placed Photios in the patriarchal seat.

7 It should be noted that some think the letters "sha" and "tsi" were based instead on Armenian or Samaritan letters. That doesn't change the creation story, as Cyril would have encountered each language on his two prior state missions.

8 The *filioque* states that the Spirit comes to humans from the Son and Father, not solely from the Father. The Roman church insisted that the *filioque* is biblically accurate. The Orthodox countered that such was not part of the original creeds. The disagreement became the major theological dispute in the Great Schism.

9 Possibly the most fascinating find in the flotsam was a pagan sarcophagus that had been re-purposed. The side opposite the pagan funerary script sported cruder carvings of a Christian burial invocation.

10 St. Cyril apparently passed from this mortal coil on February 14. Surely it would be more appropriate to celebrate him on that day instead of St. Valentine, whose quasi-legendary acts bear no resemblance to the cupidity of modern Valentine's Day. However, given the juggernaut that is Valentine's Day in the West, it seems likely St. Cyril will remain as buried under debris in celebration as he was in construction.

11 For example, Roman Catholic philosopher Peter Kreeft wrote a witty and brilliant essay in 2013 in which he listed nineteen judgments inherent in life. He apologized that he could only find nineteen, matching Frodo Baggin's number of digits. Had Dr. Kreeft understood the particular judgment or *bema* according to the Protestant theology, he could have used Bilbo as his model instead.

12 The experts are unnamed for their own protection. The concern is not with repercussions in Rome, but for their safety in hostile countries where these scholars are doing important work *incognito*.

13 In Orthodox iconography, the greatest blessing is shown when the ring finger of the right hand reaches across to touch the thumb. This shaped the hand in a kind of shorthand (no pun intended) spelling the letters IC XC, which stood for "Jesus Christ." In western Christian (Catholic) art after 500, the finger positions are less important as the art is more about narrative than icon. In general, the Catholic hand is raised open. If any digits touch the thumb, the middle or index fingers are usually employed.

14 Bedouelle, Guy, *Illustrated History of the Church: The Great Challenges*, 22.

15 www.basilcasanclemente.com viewed February 8, 2022. Note: This great work of art was practically invisible when the author first beheld it. It has only recently completed restoration and been made available for public viewing.

16 Historical novelists such as Gore Vidal, Dan Brown, and M. J. Polelle have popularized the notion of a Mithraic revival under various later emperors such as Julian the Apostate and Justinian. There is no evidence that Julian joined the mysteries; in fact, his Neoplatonism would have strained even his syncretistic view of tolerance at the addition of Mithras. If Justinian even heard of Mithraism, we have no record.

17 No one is allowed in the school anymore and the room is chained off for preservation. Nonetheless, a visitor can peer around and see many of the numerals set in niches.

18 "Living water" is a classical Mediterranean term for water that moves under its own power.

19 On Christianity's early adherents, see the wrtitings of Rodney Stark such as *Cities of God: The Real Story of How Christianity Became an Urban Movement and Conquered Rome*. San Francisco: HarperCollins, 2006 and*The Rise of Christianity: How the Obscure, Marginal Jesus Movement Became the Dominant Religious Force in the Western World in a Few Centuries*. New York: HarperOne, 1996.

20 But I want you to know, brethren, that the things *which happened* to me have actually turned out for the furtherance of the gospel, so that it has become evident to the whole palace guard, and to all the rest, that my chains are in Christ; and most of the brethren in the Lord, having become confident by my chains, are much more bold to speak the word without fear. [*Philippians* 1:12–14 New King James Version]

21 The altar one sees there now was added later.

22 One of the few things we know for certain about Latin pronunciation is that they also preferred the hard "C" sound. Indeed, Latin lacked a soft "c" sound for centuries, a fact attested by a later extant letter making fun of Iberians who have started to use a soft "c" sound.

23 Other letters attributed to Clement are suspect at best. Only *1 Clement* is widely accepted as genuine.

24 Whether Clement considered himself a bishop of Rome and whether that position conferred papal authority during the first two Christian centuries is a matter of debate. On the one hand, there is a dearth of evidence for monarchical bishops in Rome during Clement's era. On the other hand, later Christian leaders such as Tertullian (who died roughly 100 years after Clement) consider him bishop and pope.

25 Harrison, Everett F., *Romans* in the *Expositors' Bible Commentary*, 9.

26 Paul Greenwold, "Paul Engages the Roman World," 6.

This subject is dealt with on a scholarly level in many recent studies. Those wanting more data could begin with the bibliography in *Scripture, Texts, and Tracings in Romans* edited by Linda L. Belleville and A. Andrew Das.

27 *Romans* 6:22–23 Holman Christian Standard Bible.

28 *Romans* 6:17–18 Holman Christian Standard Bible.

29 *Ephesians* 2:17 Holman Christian Standard Bible.

30 Peter Lampe, *From Paul to Valentius: Christians at Rome in the First Two Centuries* (Minneapolis, MN: Fortress Press, 2003), 41–47.

31 We only address the first letter because no scholar I have read or known believes the other epistles attributed to him were actually written by St. Clement. In language, theology, and theme they appear far off the Clementine mark.

32 von Harnack, *1 Clement,* 72.

33 Ibid., 31. While Lightfoot and von Harnack authored the most influential works on *1 Clement,* recent scholarship continues to draw out interesting implications from the letter. For a general introduction with an excellent bibliography covering past discussions, see Andreas Lindemann, "The First Epistle of Clement" in *The Apostolic Fathers: An Introduction,* 47–61.

34 These are often drawn from Hebrew texts and not the Septuagint (the Greek translation of the Old Testament).

35 As F. F. Bruce summarizes in his commentary on *Romans,* "Clement… shows himself well acquainted with the letter to the Romans; he echoes its language time and again… The way in which he echoes its language suggests he knew it by heart." Bruce, *Romans,* 27. For a more technical presentation on similarities, see Chapter 6, "Clement's Use of Hebrews and the Pauline Epistles" (pages 179–237) in Donald Alfred Hagner, *The Use of the Old and New Testaments in Clement of Rome.* Leiden: Brill, 1973.

36 Elmer Truesdale Merrill, *Essays in Early Christian History,* 104.

37 F. F. Bruce, *Romans,* 57.

38 Martin Luther, *Preface to the Epistle to the Romans,* 1.

39 Like those in 1st-century Corinth and Rome, today's churches need clarity, conviction, and purity. Christians do not fully live by faith because we do not understand the depth of our need nor the grand scope of God's provision. In this age of ignorance, *Romans* and *1 Clement* teach what it means to be righteous by virtue of faith.

40 Della Porta, *Subterranean Rome* (Cambridge, UK: Goodfellow & Egan, 2000), 15.

41 Though not connected to this subject, the routing of the 20,000 dedicated pirates is a grand story. Cicero rightly praised Pompey for accomplishing what had never been previously enjoyed in the eastern Mediterranean—free and safe trade.

42 "Invincible, born out of rock" may seem an odd title, given that Mithras appeared in the sky. However, in Mithraism, the sun is considered born out of the rock that is the vault of the cosmos. Light is thus viewed as a material thing springing from the original rock of the heavens.

43 Della Porta, *Subterranean Rome,* 16–17.

44 Though Nymphs are female in Greco-Roman thought, the Mithraic use seems to have been a chrysalis formulation. The male emerges from the female "shell" just as a butterfly from the caterpillar's chrysalis.

45 Justin Martyr, *First Apology*, ch. 66.

46 Tertullian, *De praescriptione haereticorum,* 39–40.

47 *Colossians* 1:26–27 English Standard Version.

48 *John* 10:16 New American Standard Bible.

49 *Colossians* 3:1–4 Holman Christian Standard Bible.

50 Barclay, William, *Letters to the Philippians, Colossians, and Thessalonians,* 142.

51 *Romans* 5:18–21 New American Standard Bible.

52 Adkins, Lesley & Adkins, Roy, *Dictionary of Roman Religion*, 117–18.

53 Many think the repetition was memorial or ceremonial and did not involve physical blood after the first baptism. Others declare that live bulls were always used, and for proof point to the remains in the Mithraeum under the Circus Maximus. On the exclusion of women, see Jonathan David, "The Exclusion of Women in the Mithraic Mysteries: Ancient or Modern?" *Numen* 47:2 (2000), 121–41.

54 Pelikan, Jaroslav, *The Emergence of the Catholic Tradition*, p. 2.

55 *1 Timothy* 6:20–21 Christian Standard Bible.

56 *1 John* 5:21 Christian Standard Bible.

BIBLIOGRAPHY

Classical and Early Sources

Clement of Rome, *Epistles of 1 and 2 Clement* (see below under editors)

Eusebius, *Ecclesiastical History*

Jerome, *Episteolae ad Laetam*

Justin Martyr, *First Apology*

Ignatius, *De praescriptione haereticorum*

Tertullian, *De Corona*

Contemporary Sources

Adkins, Lesley and Roy A. Adkins. *Dictionary of Roman Religion*. New York: Facts on File, 1995.

Adkins, Lesley and Roy A. Adkins. *Handbook to Life in Ancient Rome*. Rev. ed. New York: Oxford University Press, 1998.

Alessandroni, Maria Gabriella and Remedia, Gianrenzo. "The Most Severe Floods of the Tiber River in Rome" in *The Extremes of the Extremes: Extraordinary Floods* (Proceedings of a symposium held at Reykjavik. Iceland. July 2000).

Andrews, Frank (psedu.). *Ancient Slavs*. Stevens Point, WI: Worzalla Publishing Company, 1976.

Barclay, William. *Letters to the Philippians, Colossians, and Thessalonians.* 3rd ed. Louisville, KY: Westminster John Knox Press, 2003.

Bedouelle, Guy. *Illustrated History of the Church: The Great Challenges.* Chicago: Liturgy Training Publications, 2006.

Belleville, Linda L. and Das, A. Andrew, editors. *Scripture, Texts, and Tracings in Romans.* Minneapolis, MN: Lexington Books/Fortress Academic, 2021.

Boyce, Mary and Grenet, Franz. *Zoroastrianism under Macedonian and Roman Rule.* Leiden: E. J. Brill, 2015.

Boyle, Kane, Guidobaldi. *San Clemente Miscellany 2: Art and Archaeology.* Rome: Apud S. Clementum, 1978.

Boyle, Leonard. *A Short Guide to St. Clement's Rome.* Rome: Collegio San Clemente, 1989.

Brilliant, Virginia. "Envisaging the Particular Judgment in Late-Medieval Italy" *Speculum* Vol. 84, No. 2 (Apr., 2009): 314–46.

Bruce, F. F. *Paul: Apostle of the Heart Set Free.* Carlisle, Cumbria, UK: Paternoster Press, 1977.

Bruce, F. F. *Romans.* Downers Grove, IL: InterVarsity Press, 1985.

Cary, M. and H. H. Scullard. *A History of Rome: Down to the Reign of Constantine.* New York: Macmillan, 1975.

Chadwick, Henry. *Early Christian Thought and The Classical Tradition: Studies in Justin, Clement, and Origen.* Oxford, UK: Oxford University Press, 1966.

Cilliers, Breytenbach, and Laurence L. Welborn, ed.. *Encounters with Hellenism: Studies on the First Letter of Clement.* Leiden: Brill, 2006.

Claridge, Amanda. *Rome.* Oxford Archaeological Oxford Guides. New York: Oxford University Press, 1998.

Cochrane, Charles. *Christianity and Classical Culture: A Study of Thought and Action from Augustus to Augustine.* Reprint ed. Indianapolis, IN: Liberty Fund, 2003.

Coulston, John and Dodge, Hazel. *Ancient Rome: The Archaeology of the Eternal City* Oxford: Oxford University School of Archaeology, 2000.

Cumont, Franz translated by Thomas J. McCormack. *The Mysteries of Mithra*

David, Jonathan. "The Exclusion of Women in the Mithraic Mysteries: Ancient or Modern?" *Numen* 47:2 (2000): 121–41.

de la Bédoyère, Guy, *Praetorian: The Rise and Fall of Rome's Imperial Bodyguard.* New Haven, CT: Yale University Press, 2017.

de Rossi, Giovanni Battista. *La Roma Sotterranea Cristiana* 3 vol. Rome: Chromo-lithografia Pontificia, 1864.

Dittrich, Zdenek Radslav. *Christianity in Great-Moravia.* Groningen: J. B. Wolters, 1962.

Goldsworthy, Adrian. *Pax Romana: War, Peace, and Conquest in the Roman World.* New Haven, CT: Yale University Press, 2017.

Grant, Michael. *The Twelve Caesars.* New York: Charles Scribner's Sons, 1975.

Greenwold, Doug. "Paul Engages the Roman World" a paper presented at The Institute of Biblical Context Conference, Zeeland, Michigan, June 11, 2019.

Hagner, Donald Alfred. *The Use of the Old and New Testaments in Clement of Rome*. Leiden: Brill, 1973.

Harrison, Everett F. "Romans" *in The Expositors' Bible Commentary, Volume 10: Romans through Galatians*. Grand Rapids, MI: Zondervan, 1977.

Joshel, Sandra H. *Slavery in the Roman World*. Cambridge: University of Cambridge Press, 2010.

Kertzer, David. *The Kidnapping of Edgardo Mortara*. New York: Vintage Books, 1998.

King, William Leslie. *Investment and Achievement: A Study in Christian Progress*. Sydney, Aust: Wentworth Press, 2016.

Krautheimer, Richard and Ćurčić, Slobodan. *Early Christian and Byzantine Architecture*. New Haven, CT: Yale University Press, 1987.

Lampe, Peter. *From Paul to Valentius: Christians at Rome in the First Two Centuries*. Minneapolis, MN: Fortress Press, 2003.

Lightfoot, J. B. *The Apostolic Fathers*. 4 vol. Peabody, MA: Hendrickson Publishers, 1989.

Lindemann, Andreas. "The First Epistle of Clement." In *The Apostolic Fathers: An Introduction*. Edited by Wilhelm Pratscher, Waco, TX: Baylor University Press, 2010.

Lloyd, Joan E. Barclay. "The Building History of the Medieval Church of S. Clemente in Rome" *Journal of the Society of Architectural Historians* 45:3 (1986): 197–223.

Luther, Martin. *Preface to the Epistle to the Romans,* New Creation Publications, Adelaide, 2003.

Mancinelli, Fabrizio. *Catacombs of Rome and the Origins of Christianity.* London: Scala, 1998.

Markchies, Christoph. "Harnack's Image of 1 Clement and Contemporary Research", in: *Zeitschrift für Antikes Christentum* 18 (2014): 54–69.

Melville-Jones, John. "The Location of the Trajanic Mint at Rome," *The Numismatic Chronicle* Vol. 175, (2015): 137–45.

Merrill, Elmer Truesdale. *Essays in Early Christian History.* London: MacMillan & Co., Ltd., 1924.

Mullooly, Joseph. *St. Clement Pope and Martyr and his Basilica in Rome.* Rome: G. Barbera, 1873.

Osborne, John. *Early Mediaeval Wall-Paintings in the Lower Church of San Clemente.* New York: Garland Publishing, 1984.

Papandrea, James L. *Rome: A Pilgrim's Guide to the Eternal City,* Eugene, OR: Cascade Books, 2012.

Pearcey, Nancy. *Saving Leonardo.* Nashville: B&H Publishing, 2010.

Pelikan, Jaroslav. *Jesus Through the Centuries.* New Haven, CT: Yale University Press, 1999.

Pelikan, Jaroslav. *The Christian Tradition: A History of the Development of Doctrine, Vol. 1, The Emergence of the Catholic Tradition*. Chicago: The University of Chicago Press, 1975.

Della, Porta. *Subterranean Rome*. Cambridge, UK: Goodfellow & Egan, 2000.

Portella, Ivanna, and Smith, Mark E., et al. *Subterranean Rome*. New York: Könemann, 2005.

Ramsay, Sir William M. *The Church in the Roman Empire before A.D. 170*. New York: G. P. Putnam's Sons, 1893.

Riasanovsky, Nicholas and Mark D. Steinberg. *A History of Russia. 9th ed*. New York: Oxford University Press, 2018.

Rutgers, L. V. *Subterranean Rome*. Leuven: Peeters Publishers, 2000.

Sell, Alice. *Grand Duchess of Hesse, Princess of Great Britain and Ireland, Biographical Sketch and Letters* (1885). Reprint ed. Whitefish, MT, 2010.

Smalley, William. *Translation as Mission: Bible Translation in the Modern Missionary Movement*. Macon, GA: Mercer University Press, 1991.

Stark, Rodney. *Cities of God: The Real Story of How Christianity Became an Urban Movement and Conquered Rome*. San Francisco: HarperCollins, 2006.

Stark, Rodney. *The Rise of Christianity: How the Obscure, Marginal Jesus Movement Became the Dominant Religious Force in the Western World in a Few Centuries*. New York: HarperOne, 1996.

Steele, Dorman, ed.. *Barnes' Brief History of Rome.* New York: Chautuaqua Press, 1885.

Urbanus, Jason. "Rome's Imperial Port," *Archaeology Magazine* (March/April 2015): 26–33.

von Harnack, Adolf. *An Introduction to Early Christianity: The Letter from the Roman Church to the Corinthian Church during the era of Domitian (1st Letter of Clement): Translated and Explained for Students [Einführung in die Alte Kirchengeschichte: Das Schreiben der römischen Kirche an die korinthische aus der Zeit Domitians (I. Clemensbrief) übersetzt und den Studierenden erklärt* ; "Der erste Klemensbrief: Eine Studie zur Bestimmung des Charakters des ältesten Heidenchristentums," *Sitzungsberichte der Preußischen Akademie der Wissenschaften: Philosophisch-historische Klasse*

von Harnack, Adolph. *1 Clement.* Leipzig: J. C. Hinrichs'sche Buchhandlung, 1929.

Webb, Matilda. *The Churches and Catacombs of Early Christian Rome: A Comprehensive Guide.* Eastbourne, UK: Sussex Academic Press, 2001.

Welborn, Laurence L. "The Preface to 1 Clement: The Rhetorical Situation and the Traditional Date," in *Encounters with Hellenism: Studies on the First Letter of Clement.* Leiden: Brill, 2020.

Young, Norwood. *The Story of Rome.* London: J. M. Dent & Co., 1901.

Interview

Father Dr. Paul Lawlor, personal interview by Wayne Braudrick, May, 2006.

Websites

www.basilcasanclemente.com

https://thepaideiablog.wordpress.com/2014/11/23/the-fresco-of-sisinnius-and-st-clement/

ACKNOWLEDGMENTS

Once again, my appreciation grows for Dr. Tim Demy and Stone Tower Press. Thanks are also due Carolyn Powell and Katya Braudrick, my wonderfully perfectionist copy editors, and Janna Braudrick for the excellent photos. (Note: her pictures were taken years before the site director banned photography.)

The Forge Guild, headed by Matt Lantz, Jake Collins, and Katelyn Sullins, spent a wonderful day with me at St. Clements and helped motivate me to finish this work. Dr. Sandra Glahn of Dallas Theological Seminary encouraged the work as well, both with her early manuscript reading and the famous 3 a.m. Zoom teaching session with her travelers. As mentioned in the text, Dr. Paul Lawlor was an invaluable guide, along with the priests who remain unnamed.

Of course, nothing would move forward without the wonderful team at All The Difference. Finally, I praise God for my family. Janna, Kris, Reuben, Chip, Jessica, Grant, Michael, Katya, and Benjamin all surrendered time so this could be completed. Thank you.

ABOUT THE AUTHOR

Wayne Braudrick, PhD, serves as Senior Pastor of Frisco Bible Church. A frequent visitor to Rome and tour guide of Christian sites in Rome, he also serves as adjunct faculty for Ouachita Baptist University and teaches through the All the Difference daily podcast/radio broadcast. Dr. Braudrick earned his doctorate from Middlesex University in London; earned a master's degree in Bible at Dallas Theological Seminary, and was a National Merit Scholar at Baylor University where he read history, literature, and education.

NOTES

NOTES